ROMANTIC N.Y.

*165 Romantic Things
to See and Do in New York*

MARILYN APPLEBERG

An Apple Ink, Ltd. Book
in Association with G&H Soho, Inc.

ACKNOWLEDGMENTS

Gratitude to Thomas P. Roche for his invaluable research assistance and unabashed love of NY, Charles Levine for his encouragement, Jim Harris and Gerry Burstein for their faith, and Fran Bartlett and Christina Viera for their hard work.

Excerpt from "Recuerdo" by Edna St. Vincent Millay. From Collected Poems, HarperCollins. Copyright 1922, 1950 by Edna St. Vincent Millay. Reprinted by permission of Elizabeth Barnett, literary executor.

Excerpt from "To Brooklyn Bridge" by Hart Crane. From COMPLETE POEMS OF HART CRANE by Marc Simon, editor. Copyright 1933, © 1958, 1966, by Liveright Publishing Corporation. Copyright © 1986 by Marc Simon. Reprinted by permission of Liveright Publishing Corporation.

TRY TO REMEMBER, by Tom Jones, Harvey Schmidt
© 1960 (Renewed) Tom Jones & Harvey Schmidt
Chappell & Co., owner of Publication and Allied Rights
All Rights Reserved. Used by Permission
WARNER BROS. PUBLICATIONS U.S. INC., Miami, FL 33014

Apple Ink, Ltd.
c/o G&H Soho, Inc.
70 Hudson Street
Hoboken, NJ 07030

ISBN 0-9605188-2-7

Library of Congress Cataloging-in-Publication Data has been applied for.

Romantic N.Y. is available at special discount for bulk purchase for sales promotions, premiums, fund-raising, or educational use. For details contact:
Jim Harris
G&H Soho, Inc. (201) 216–9400; FAX (201) 216–1778

Extreme care has been taken to ensure that all information in this book is accurate and up to date, but the publisher cannot be held responsible for any errors that may appear.

Printed in the United States of America

I dedicate this book to the memory of my dear friend Peter Allen, who I believe now resides forever between the moon and New York City.

CONTENTS

INTRODUCTION

How can New York be thought of as anything but romantic? What other place occupies the dreams of so many who are from somewhere else and yearn to be here? What other city behaves so much like a lover? Where else is the unexpected the norm?

New York exasperates, frustrates, disappoints, confounds, but just as quickly, and blessedly more often, New York delights, enchants, and seduces. E.B. White compared the city to an illusive poem imbued with magic. It's a city to be in love with . . . and to be in love in.

Even though this book is not for lovers only, we all know that being in love in New York is a double delight. Suddenly you savor the crystal clear night when the lights of the city seem a part of a celestial sky show; the first gentle snowfall when your childhood appears to beckon; that mist-shrouded evening when the city's hard edges are softened. It's when New York becomes more of itself and yet is also everywhere else lovers might want to be. So the two of you seek out the little bistro so reminiscent of Paris, that market with the aura of Arles, the grotto-like garden that conjures up Rome. Where else but New York could you go so many places without leaving this handful of islands?

But the special romance of New York resides in its inherent ability to transform itself—and you—between every sunrise and sunset, every sunset and sunrise. The Romance of New York is everywhere, especially within the covers of this book.

I confess that I have used the word "romantic" nearly 100 times in *Romantic N.Y.* Just as there is no true substitute for the feeling, there is no suitable synonym for the word.

Marilyn Appleberg
New York, 1996

ROMANTIC QUICK PICKS

The following specialized indexes are designed to help you quickly zero in on a specific romantic aspect of the city, for those times when you want to primarily see the sunset, cap an evening, be dazzled by a view, warmed by a fireplace, dine outdoors, have a picnic, or listen to live music. They are all here for the picking.

Places to Be at Sunset

Restaurants & Bars

Working Fireplaces

Picnic Times and Places

NEW YORK STATE
OF MIND

1

There are places in this city that don't transport you elsewhere, they are quintessentially New York, and are to be embraced, savored, and appreciated, for exactly that reason. Each is imbued with the spirit of this city, and their meaning far transcends their ordinary daily use. After all, what is a bridge but a means of getting from one place to another, a train station, no longer used for long-distance travel, or an office building, no longer the world's tallest. Yet, each of them—the Brooklyn Bridge, Grand Central Terminal, the Empire State Building—as well as the others in this chapter is a symbol of a time when the country was young and this city was a magnet for those who dared to dream. These places say New York to all who see their images, and to some they say America. They serve to confirm New York's place in history, at the same time giving its present a note of grace, beauty, and timelessness. Natives take them for granted, to be brought forward from the back of the mind only when out-of-towners come to visit. Take this unabashed romantic New Yorker's word for it, they are each—when visited at the right time, in the right frame of mind, and with the right person—extremely romantic.

The Brooklyn Bridge

O sleepless as the river under thee,
Vaulting the sea, the prairies' dreaming sod,
Unto us lowliest sometime sweep, descend
And of the curveship lend a myth to God.

Hart Crane, "To Brooklyn Bridge"

The bridge, an aesthetic and technical marvel, celebrated its 100th birthday in 1983, and the city hosted a huge birthday bash in its honor, a romantic notion in and of itself. Though now dwarfed by the buildings surrounding it, the bridge's grace and strength remain unmatched. Few manmade structures in modern times have enjoyed such devoted attention by artists, writers, poets, and photographers as the Brooklyn Bridge.

The Great Bridge, as it was called when it was built, was the first to boast a pedestrian promenade, and the one-mile-plus-a-bit walk across it is still downright dramatic. Stroll across the bridge, and you will be thrilled by the skylines of Manhattan and Brooklyn and by the view of the harbor through the filigree web of cables. And you will appreciate just how successful its builder, Washington Roebling, was in combining engineering skill and vision with poetic beauty. Roebling, who was severely debilitated during the building of the bridge, relied on his wife Emily to carry his instructions to those engaged in its construction. It was she who first rode triumphantly across the finished bridge in May 1883, carrying with her a live rooster as a symbol of victory, with Roebling watching from their Columbia Heights house through a telescope. He had not been to the bridge in fourteen years, nor, I was told by his great grandson in 1983, did he *ever* cross it. A plaque on the bridge honors Emily Roebling, without whom the project would not have gone forward. Theirs was an epic love story, and the bridge is its legacy.

The day the Great Bridge opened 150,300 pedestrians paid a penny to cross it. It was awe-inspiring then, and though the view today is not quite so expansive, it is still awesome—and free.

Brooklyn Bridge, from Park Row (look for the sign "Bridge Footpath") in Manhattan to Cadman Plaza West in Brooklyn Heights.

P.S. If you are coming from Brooklyn, time your walk for sunset to see the skyline bathed in pale pinks and purple as the sun descends behind the buildings of Lower Manhattan. Then reward yourselves with a drink at the Harbour Lights Restaurant, on Pier 17 (third floor) at the South Street Seaport where you can continue to contemplate the bridge, now aglow against the night sky, from its romantic outdoor deck. If you walk from Manhattan, have a drink at the River Café (#155) and enjoy the amazing view and then take a shorter walk along the five-block Brooklyn Heights promenade (#63) for another gorgeous gander at Gotham. If the two of you prefer an escort, join one of the twilight tours of the Brooklyn Bridge and Brooklyn Heights offered May to October by Big Onion Walking Tours (212)439-1090. The cost is $9.

THE EMPIRE STATE BUILDING

THE EMPIRE STATE BUILDING has been an indelible landmark on the New York horizon since 1931. Though at 1,250 feet it's no longer the tallest building in the world, it is still, without argument, the most elegant. A steady stream of tourists ascends to the observatories throughout the day, but take a tip from this romantic and save the best for last. The observatories are open until midnight and this is the perfect spot to cap an evening. It's a time when only a handful of others, both tourists and natives, remain to share the incomparable panorama. The 86th floor provides a wrap-around outdoor terrace, the city beneath offers up the drama, and a faint roar is audible even at this height. It's awfully romantic.

The enclosed 102nd-floor aerie is as high as you can get, and though the view is not appreciably better from here, forty-something movie buffs may recall that this is where Cary Grant waited in vain for Deborah Kerr in the 1958 film *An Affair to Remember*, a movie memory revived in the sentimental 1993 hit *Sleepless in Seattle*. At closing time allow everyone else to leave ahead of you so you can linger—this is the most romantic moment of all. Toast it with the split of champagne you had the forethought to bring. The last time I was there a couple was celebrating their first wedding anniversary—they had met in the building's elevator. Honest!

Empire State Building, 350 Fifth Avenue at 34th Street. (212)736-3100. OPEN 7 days 9:30 AM to midnight; the last elevator up is at 11:30 PM. Admission $4.

P.S. If you are planning to be married on Valentine's Day, consider having the ceremony here if you don't mind sharing the spotlight with others who have the same idea; call (212)736-3100, ext. 337 for details. Of course, there is nothing to prevent you from taking your vows at the Empire State Building any day of the year as long as you pay the admission.

Grand Central Terminal

TRAIN STATIONS as they were built at the turn of the century are inherently romantic places, conceived as they were to be grand entryways to modern metropolises. Grand Central Terminal, designed in 1913 to be nothing less than the "gateway to a continent," is by that definition even more romantic. Though the station today is used by commuter lines only, the building itself has taken center stage following its rescue and subsequent designation as a landmark. The Municipal Art Society, instrumental in its deliverance, leads a fascinating one-hour free tour every Wednesday at 12:30 PM, of the majestic building, which includes visits to some secret places you would never know existed. It is a great lunchtime rendezvous, under the guise of checking out a couple of the building's architectural nooks and crannies.

Tour highlights include an elevator ride (from the left of the Vanderbilt Avenue and East 44th Street entrance) to the top, where four stories above the grand cathedral-like main concourse there is a little-used catwalk that runs the width of the building. Walking out onto it gives an unusual perspective of the crowds below, not to mention a place to kiss in public without being seen! Another interesting tidbit revealed on the tour is the "whispering corner," located just outside the Oyster Bar restaurant on the lower level. There in the corners of the arched area you can whisper into the wall, and the person standing in the corner diagonally across from you can hear clearly what you say.

But the most romantic thing you can do in New York's grandest public space is waltz across the vast concourse — for true romantics doable anytime, of course, but with a live orchestra and other couples, you have to wait for New Year's Eve. Dancing in the terminal is one of the landmark events of New York's First Night New Year's Eve Celebration.

Grand Central Terminal, East 42nd Street and Vanderbilt Avenue. The Grand Central tour gathers in front of the Chemical Bank Commuter Express every Wednesday at 12:30 PM; for more information call (212)935-3960. For information about the First Night New Year's Eve Celebration, call (212)922-9393. If you're hungry after the tour, have some great chowder or an oyster sampler in the Oyster Bar, a landmark on the lower level since 1915.

P.S. The Café Grand Central on the west balcony overlooking the main concourse is an interesting and well-located place to meet someone in midtown for a drink and people-watching after work before moving on for the evening.

THE METROPOLITAN MUSEUM OF ART

4 THE METROPOLITAN MUSEUM, one of the world's greatest repositories of fine arts, takes on an added identity after 5 o'clock on Friday and Saturday, when it resembles nothing less than a small European city at that delicious time between night and day. It's a time to be savored, especially at week's end, by taking a leisurely promenade, sitting at a café, being alone, or socializing with one or more. At the Met you may do any and all of the above in the company of Caravaggio, Rodin, Rembrandt, Van Gogh, and Brueghel.

The Metropolitan is much more than the sum of its parts, and with the new evening hours it's one of the classiest spots in town to have a cocktail. Whether on your own or with someone special, it's magical, especially in summer when the rest of the city is in the throes of leaving town. The lobby is festive, music wafts down from overhead, and, yes, that's the sound of clinking glasses. Go to the softly lighted balcony overlooking the Great Hall, sit at a little cocktail table replete with tablecloth and votive candle, order a drink, nibble on the tastiest pretzels in town, and listen to Vivaldi and Mozart played by a Juilliard quintet. You may linger as long as you wish, but when and if you can tear yourself away (perhaps you've made a new friend by now) float through your favorite old or new gallery. And even if you've seen it before, don't miss the Temple of Dendur, never more dramatic than at dusk, positively haunting later in the evening. Your next stop should be the Iris and B. Gerald Cantor Roof Garden. Open from May to October, weather permitting, the lovely outdoor exhibit features several large Rodin sculptures with the elegant skyline and Central Park as a breathtaking backdrop. A small bar here serves alfresco cocktails. It's perfect at twilight and particularly striking in the fall, when the park around you is in full glorious color.

OPEN Sunday and Tuesday through Thursday 9:30 AM to 5:15 PM, Friday and Saturday untill 8:45 PM. Drinks accompanied by music are served on the balcony Friday and Saturday from 4:45 PM till closing. Suggested museum contribution $7.

P.S. The museum dining room is open till 10 PM on Friday and Saturday, and with candlelight and a classical guitarist it too takes on a romantic glow. On a budget? There is a self-service cafeteria on the periphery of the restaurant, as well as an espresso café/bar.

Great New York Summer Date: On a gentle summer evening approach the museum through Central Park. Enter at East 72nd Street and stop for a drink at the Boathouse Café (#133) before visiting the Met—or start with cocktails at the museum followed by dinner at the Boathouse.

THE PLAZA HOTEL

THE PLAZA HOTEL, like most New Yorkers, has had it ups and downs in recent years. But thanks to the Donald (Trump, that is) and his former wife Ivana, the Plaza built in 1907 is once again up. I have to confess, though, even in the down years the Plaza occupied a special place in my romantic repertoire, where I understood exactly what Hemingway meant when he advised F. Scott Fitzgerald to bequeath his liver to Princeton but his heart to the Plaza.

Fitzgerald and his wife Zelda danced out of the hotel one evening in the 1920s and proceeded fully clothed into the Pulitzer Fountain across the plaza, becoming forever a part of the hotel's legend.

When the Savoy Plaza, across Fifth Avenue, was demolished to make way for the eyesore that is the General Motors Building, I boldly swore that if the Plaza were ever to suffer the same fate I would be compelled to leave New York, forever. Whew! Henry J. Hardenbergh's splendid French Renaissance chateau is now a city and National Historic Landmark, and I have been saved from self-imposed exile. The Plaza and New York are indelibly intertwined, and now as long as there is one there will be the other.

Elsewhere the rooms may be larger, the service better, or prices lower, but the Plaza's exuberant architecture, legendary past, and fortuitous location on a spacious plaza across from Central Park make it a sentimental favorite. Even if you don't plan to stay, have afternoon tea in the Palm Court (#32), an after-work cocktail in the Oak Bar (#117), or a twilight dinner in the grandeur of the Edwardian Room. Who knows, maybe then you will be ordering a room. Remember, too, Tiffany's is nearby (#96).

The Plaza Hotel, Fifth Avenue and 58th Street. (212)759-3000.

P.S. The Plaza offers a variety of well-priced weekend packages, some with champagne and other romantic extras included; call for a brochure. FYI: The bridal suite, No. 1011, rents for $1,200 per night.

9

THE STATEN ISLAND FERRY

We were very tired, we were very merry,
We had gone back and forth all night on the ferry.

Edna St. Vincent Millay

WHETHER ON A DATE or on your own, a wonderful spot you will find to renew your love affair with New York as well as promote a more personal alliance is from the outside deck of the Staten Island Ferry as it moves away from Manhattan. The best time is at twilight in the fall or winter when the air is clear and the skyline makes a show of turning pale shades of mauve and pink, becoming almost mirage-like, seeming to melt into the water. It's a spectacular viewpoint, *and* a romantic one. On the return trip thirty minutes later the skyline will have come back to life — night life, that is — all aglow, radiating light and energy. Your heart will stir, and if you are at all open to the wonder of this city, you will once more realize that this is what all the fuss is about. Fifty cents is a small price to pay for such a grand gift.

Note: More unromantic you cannot get than the terminal at St. George, Staten Island; take heart, you are there for only a short time.

The Staten Island Ferry Terminal is at the foot of Whitehall Street, Battery Park (718)727-2508. Boats leave every half hour on weekdays, every hour on weekends except between 11 AM and 7 PM. Avoid rush hours.

P.S. You will no doubt feel invigorated by the view, and you'll probably be hungry, so head over to nearby Chinatown for a meal. If you wish to make more of your trip to Staten Island, see #79 for things to see and do.

ROMANTIC
GRAB BAG

*T*here are many things to see and do in New York that defy categorization. They present a myriad of opportunities to feel and be romantic at various times during the day and night; some are expensive, some are inexpensive, and some are free. Like a handful of snowflakes, they are all quite different from one another, but together they cover the landscape—so much so that you will wonder how any of them ever got by you.

AMERICAN MUSEUM OF NATURAL HISTORY

7 THERE MAY NOT BE ANYTHING ROMANTIC about tyrannosaurs (except think Cary Grant and Katharine Hepburn in *Bringing Up Baby*), but the museum's Hall of Minerals and Gems with nearly $50 million worth of glitter on display is enough to start any heart beating a bit faster. Have a look at the 87.64-carat engraved emerald believed to have been worn by a Hindu princess more than 300 years ago. Here too, is the 563-carat Star of India sapphire, which was stolen from the museum in a daring 1964 jewel heist and subsequently recovered. How's that for intrigue and romance!

But for a real adventure head for the Hall of Ocean Life, a cavernous space dramatically lit to simulate the bottom of the sea. Look up at the massive 94-foot fiberglass replica of a mammoth blue whale that hangs suspended from the ceiling. For maximum romantic effect go on a Friday or Saturday, when right under the blue whale the Whale's Lair Lounge is open until 8 o'clock for drinks and snacks. Imbibe its namesake concoction, a sweet lethal blend of vodka, pineapple juice, and blue curaçao, and you'll feel as if you've been swept away. There's no other cocktail lounge like it in the city—perhaps in the world.

American Museum of Natural History, Central Park West at West 79th Street. (212)769-5100. OPEN Sunday through Thursday 10 AM to 5:45 PM, Friday and Saturday until 8:45 PM. Suggested museum admission $7. The Whale's Lair Cocktail Lounge is OPEN Friday 3 PM to 8 PM, Saturday noon to 8 PM, and Sunday noon to 5 PM.

13

FORBES MAGAZINE GALLERIES

MALCOLM FORBES was a millionaire who knew how to have a good time (remember his birthday bash in Morocco?), and his tiny namesake museum located on the ground floor of the Forbes Magazine Building, which displays the playthings of a time long past, is a tribute to that side of his nature. It's a unique space where more than 500 toy boats and 12,000 miniature tin and lead figures are charmingly arrayed. Also here, testimony to Forbes's extravagance, is his collection of fabulous Fabergé eggs, made by the legendary jeweler for Czar Nicholas of Russia as gifts to his beloved Czarina, Alexandra. Forbes first became acquainted with Fabergé's work when he purchased a gold cigarette case for his wife; other *objets de luxe* followed. From 1885 through 1916, fifty-four imperial eggs were commissioned, and forty-three of them are known to have survived. This collection, containing eleven of the fabled eggs, is second only to that of Britain's Queen Elizabeth II; ten eggs remain in Russia. They are extraordinary examples of craftsmanship, artistic beauty, and luxurious indulgence in the name of love.

Forbes Magazine Galleries, 62 Fifth Avenue between 12th and 13th Streets. (212)620-2389. OPEN Tuesday through Saturday 10 AM to 4 PM (Thursday is reserved for groups). Free.

BARGEMUSIC

PREMIER CLASSICAL MUSICAL EVENTS are staged against a panorama of Manhattan skyscrapers in the air-conditioned hull of this small wooden former coffee barge docked near the base of the Brooklyn Bridge. The gentle rocking of the moored boat provides an added dimension to "Chamber Music with a Different View," performed every Thursday year-round at 7:30 PM, in winter Sunday at 4 PM, and in summer Friday at 7:30 PM. What's more, in both winter and summer during intermission you can watch the sun set over Manhattan from the deck of this unique concert venue. The ambiance is favorable for romance, and after the performance just follow the feeling next door to the River Café (#155) for a drink, and then continue on for a stroll along the Brooklyn Heights promenade (#63).

Bargemusic, Fulton Ferry Landing, Brooklyn. (718)624-4061. Call for schedule, reservations and directions.

P.S. Ask about the Candlelight Concerts at Bargemusic, which include cocktails, buffet supper, and dessert at intermission. The cost is $100, a portion of which is tax-deductible. Note too that the barge may be rented and is often used for weddings by romantic New Yorkers.

UNION SQUARE GREENMARKET

10)

UNION SQUARE, a year-round market, provides a close-up opportunity to see, smell, and taste the changing of the seasons—no small task in a concrete jungle. It's a happy place, where New Yorkers feel close to nature and can still go to the theater in the evening. Reminiscent of the colorful food markets of Paris, Rome, and Provence, going to the farmer's market is something of a social event—what a visit to Gristede's can only imagine itself to be. There's a vicarious pleasure about it. If you can't get to the farm, at least you can meet the farmer. It's as close to the earth as some New Yorkers ever get.

Early Saturday morning before the crowds descend is the best time to go, especially on a nippy fall day when the air is perfumed with cloves, cinnamon, and hot apple cider, and colorful chrysanthemums, squash, and pumpkins dazzle the eye. It's an inspired way to begin a Saturday evening dinner at home: Together you can shop, prepare, cook, and relish.

Greenmarket, Union Square Park, West 17th Street between Park Avenue South and Union Square West. OPEN year-round Monday, Wednesday, Friday, and Saturday 8 AM to 6 PM.

P.S. If you need to warm up, just a few steps from the Greenmarket is the City Bakery, 22 East 17th Street, (212)366-1414. Though unromantically stark, it's a great spot to get wonderfully flavorful hot soup and delicious focaccia, or enticing and comforting hot chocolate with fresh whipped cream. They even host an annual hot chocolate festival during the month of February, featuring hot chocolate outrageously flavored with bourbon, banana peel, chili pepper, and vanilla bean. Or simply have a great cup of coffee with one of the bakery's sweet temptations.

JAMAICA BAY RIDING ACADEMY

11

THIS RIDING ACADEMY, situated on 300 acres of land in the Gateway National Park, is a well-regarded spot for riding lessons. But the most romantic aspect of the academy is the moonlight rides it features year-round every Tuesday and Thursday evening from 6:30 to 9 PM. Capable riders may go off on their own; others join the guided trail ride through woods and on a sandy beach along the shoreline of Jamaica Bay. Each season casts its own romantic spell—the vista is most beautiful in spring and fall, yet memorably stark in winter. In summer, it's a wonderful way to escape from the heat of the city. I'm told that more than a few marriage proposals have been prompted by these moonlit excursions, which in a few cases have led to weddings on horseback!

Jamaica Bay Riding Academy, 7000 Shore Parkway, Brooklyn. (718)531-8949. OPEN year-round daily 9:30 AM to 5 PM, Tuesday and Thursday 6:30 to 9 PM as well. Snack bar and tack shop on site.

PIERPONT MORGAN LIBRARY

12 THE MORGAN LIBRARY is one of the city's most alluring places. The original building, a marble-columned, marble-floored Italian Renaissance palazzo designed by McKim, Mead & White and built in 1906 for J. Pierpont Morgan, a prince of finance, is surprisingly intimate and inviting. The East Room, Morgan's own private library, with its decorated ceiling and bronze and walnut bookshelves, is one of the world's most beautiful rooms, in which items from the library's collection of printed books, bindings, and manuscripts are displayed on a rotating basis. The recent acquisition of the adjacent nineteenth-century forty-five-room brownstone, the former residence of Morgan's son J. P. Morgan, Jr., makes the complex an even more spectacular place in which to spend an hour or an entire afternoon. In the graceful, soaring glass-enclosed garden atrium, the Morgan Court Café is an enchanting and tranquil spot for light lunch, a civilized afternoon tea, or coffee and dessert.

Pierpont Morgan Library, 29 East 36th Street at Madison Avenue. (212)685-0610. OPEN Tuesday through Friday 10:30 AM to 5 PM, Saturday 10:30 AM to 6 PM, Sunday noon to 6 PM. Suggested contribution $5. Morgan Court Café OPEN Tuesday through Friday 11 AM to 4 PM, Saturday 11 AM to 5 PM, Sunday noon to 5 PM.

P.S. With a private letter of introduction and an appointment, one can see the love letters of Napoleon to Josephine and those of Byron to his mistress.

CARRIAGE HORSE RIDE

THE SOUND OF HORSE HOOFS clip-clopping on cobblestones, the trees rustling in the breeze in the summer still or winter chill of the night. Where? Right here, in New York. The promise of romance is realized when you take a hansom cab ride through Central Park, especially in late fall, covered with a blanket, when snuggling is to be expected.

Carriages are located at the southern end of Central Park (59th Street) between Fifth and Eighth Avenues. Prices should be posted.

P.S. If you take the ride anywhere other than Central Park, be it the theater district, the Lincoln Center area, or anywhere else where there are cars you are missing the point. There is nothing romantic about New York traffic fumes or a dead horse.

THE TENTH STREET RUSSIAN AND TURKISH BATHS

IF THE TWO OF YOU find harmless adventure a bonding experience, then the Russian Baths should work better than Krazy Glue. It opened over 100 years ago, and the neighborhood in which it is located has undergone some dramatic changes but still people come—zaftigs and trendies, rock stars and rabbis, cops and carpenters, models and secretaries. In the Roaring Twenties there was a room in which to check Tommy guns, and in the decades that followed clients included Frank Sinatra, John F. Kennedy, and John Belushi. Wednesday is for women only and Thursday and Sunday for men only, but new Russian owners have instituted co-ed days for the rest of the week. Couples (in bathing suits) can opt for the Turkish steam room, then a dip in the 40-degree(!) pool, and then the dry heat of the sauna, followed by a cool Swedish shower. The Russian steam bath (the *shvitz*), the star attraction, is very hot, very steamy, and very authentic. Essentially you cook on one of three rows of benches, with the uppermost the hottest; periodically you feel compelled to pour ice water from a five-gallon bucket over your head. Here you can also get a *platza*, a rubdown with a broom made of fresh oak leaves. Swedish, Shiatsu, or Russian massages are also available. In the restaurant you can have fresh carrot juice, smoked salmon, herring, fruit salad, or perhaps more appropriately a shot of Stolichnaya.

Tenth Street Russian and Turkish Baths, 268 East 10th Street between First Avenue and Avenue A. (212)473-8806. OPEN daily 9 AM to 10 PM. Admission $9. Massages are extra.

BREAKFAST AT BELMONT

FOR HORSE LOVERS who are early risers Belmont Raceway offers an opportunity to breakfast in the grandstand while watching the horses work out on the track. The track setting itself is beautifully lush in the spring and summer and particularly verdant in the fall. After the à-la-carte breakfast (hot or cold), you may take a tram ride through the stables and visit the paddock, where some of the horses will be going through their paces. It's a most unique breakfast venue.

Belmont Raceway, Belmont, Queens. (718)641-4700. Breakfast at Belmont is offered every Saturday and Sunday 7 to 9 AM when the raceway is open, approximately May through July. Parking, admission to the track, and the tour are free.

RIVERSIDE CHURCH BELL TOWER AND OBSERVATORY

FOR A CHORUS OF BELLS and a panoramic view ascend by elevator to the twentieth floor of the 392-foot tower of this imposing Upper Manhattan church. Then climb a narrow steel stairway that wends its way through the seventy-four bells of the world's largest carillon out to a windblown observation deck commanding an unparalleled 360-degree panorama. It's heavenly.

Riverside Church Bell Tower and Observatory, Riverside Drive between 120th and 122nd Streets. (212)222-5900. OPEN Monday through Saturday 11 AM to 3 PM, Sunday 12:30 to 4 PM. The Laura

Spelman Rockefeller Memorial is OPEN from 12:30 to 4 PM. The carillon is played 10:30 to 11 AM (before the 11:30 AM service), 12:30 to 1 PM, 3 to 4 PM.

P.S. To continue the bird's–eye viewing, treat yourselves to a drink or brunch or dinner at the Terrace Restaurant (#162).

THE FANTASTICKS

17 "TRY TO REMEMBER the kind of September when life was slow and oh so mellow." If you have never heard the song "Try to Remember" or "Soon It's Gonna Rain" in the context of the show for which they were written, then it's time to go. *The Fantasticks* is not a blockbuster; there are no special effects or falling chandeliers, but this simple, charming original Off Broadway musical about love found and lost and found again, which opened in Greenwich Village on May 3, 1960, has captivated a couple of generations. Go and be delighted . . . and then perhaps you'll remember.

The Fantasticks, 60 Sullivan Street. (212)674–3838. Tuesday through Friday 8 PM, Saturday 3 and 7 PM, and Sunday 3 and 7:30 PM. Tickets $35.

WHEN YOU WANT TO BE ALONE . . . TOGETHER

*T*here are places in this bustling metropolis where you can find tranquillity and beauty, where you can almost retreat, though in public, into a world of your own. These places are not secret, although some of them might as well be. Some are more centrally located than others, but they are all wonderfully accessible and rewarding in their ability to delight, transport, and make serene. They are places to escape to, to be alone in, or to visit with a special someone. To me, they are all places of the heart.

THE CLOISTERS

18

IT'S ONE OF NEW YORK'S most enchanting artistic and spiritual treasures, beautifully positioned on a high hilltop of Fort Tryon Park above the Hudson River, and it's one of the most serenely romantic places in the city. The Cloisters is a place that makes a time otherwise so remote so accessible. A branch of the Metropolitan Museum, the medieval-style structure incorporates key fragments of five French medieval monastery cloisters, a twelfth-century Spanish chapel, and a Romanesque hall.

Enter this unique environment and surrender yourself to a tranquil reverie. Recorded medieval music fills the space as you wander on your own or take a tour to view illuminated manuscripts, medieval frescoes, and the magnificent Unicorn Tapestries, handwoven in Brussels around 1500. Magnificent too are the cloistered courtyards containing over 250 species of flowers, herbs, shrubs, and trees grown in the Middle Ages in Europe; one contains plants depicted in the Unicorn Tapestries.

From the west terrace on a clear day you can revel in an uninterrupted view of the Hudson River Valley, the George Washington Bridge, and the high cliffs of the Palisades. A visit in spring is especially rapturous when the beautiful flower and fragrant herb gardens are in bloom, and there are glorious live concerts in both the spring and the fall. Or for an extraordinarily romantic interlude, make a pilgrimage to this monastery on a rainy day any time of the year.

The Cloisters is located in Fort Tryon Park. (212)923-3700. OPEN Tuesday through Sunday 9:30 AM to 5:15 PM, till 4:15 November to February. Tours every Tuesday through Friday 3 PM, Sunday noon. Suggested contribution $7.

Great New York Date: To make a memorably romantic day's outing of a visit to the Cloisters, have a picnic in Fort Tryon Park. The park, which surrounds the Cloisters and overlooks the Hudson, boasts wonderful landscaped terraces where you can have your alfresco lunch. Gaze at the Palisades across the river and inhale not only the beauty but the fragrance of lilacs, heather, tulips, and azaleas.

THE FRICK COLLECTION

THE FRICK, once the imposing city residence of the powerful steel magnate Henry Clay Frick, sits on a prized piece of urban real estate. It is one of the more civilized open-to-the-public places in New York. The residence contains Frick's personal collection of fourteenth- to nineteenth-century decorative arts, but it is the mansion itself that is an exquisite and elegant jewel. The neoclassical central garden court particularly, with its flowering begonias and ivy, Ionic columns and stone benches, is as soothing a space as can be found in Manhattan. Most days all that can be heard is the gentle sound of the water spouting from the mouths of two stone frogs within the courtyard pool, but wherever you turn in this tranquil and splendid museum there is something to delight and even surprise. (In the Fragonard Room, seek out the painting entitled *Love Letters.*) This is a repository of masterpieces built on so human a scale you never lose the feeling that this was someone's home and that in it you are an honored guest, invited to linger.

The Frick Collection, 1 East 70th Street at Fifth Avenue. (212)288-7000. OPEN Tuesday through Saturday 10 AM to 6 PM, Sunday 1 to 6 PM. Admission $5.

P.S. Classical concerts are presented in the Music Room at 5 PM on various Sundays in the spring and fall.

ISAMU NOGUCHI GARDEN MUSEUM

THE NOGUCHI MUSEUM is composed of a large, wonderfully serene, and beautiful open-air ivy-walled garden and twelve gallery spaces on two floors of what was once an engraving plant. Converted by the artist Noguchi for use as a studio, it now contains over 300 pieces of his sculpture, as well as models, drawings, and stage sets done for choreographers George Balanchine and Martha Graham.

The space as conceived by the late sculptor-designer is a unique environment for Noguchi's work, affording what are normally luxuries in the city—space, light, and time. Bamboo, a weeping cherry, and a Japanese black pine thrive in the garden's still, Zen-like environment, where a junkyard once stood. The museum is particularly striking because of its juxtaposition with the factories and warehouses that surround it. This is a worthy excursion.

Isamu Noguchi Garden Museum, 32–37 Vernon Boulevard at 33rd Road, Long Island City, Queens. (718)204-7088. OPEN April through November, Wednesday, Saturday, and Sunday 11 AM to 6 PM. Suggested contribution $4. A shuttle bus leaves every hour from the Asia Society, Park Avenue at East 70th Street, Saturday 11:30 AM to 3:30 PM. Round trip $5; call (212)721-1932. The museum is also accessible by Artlink from Roosevelt Island. The round-trip bus fare, which includes admission, is $8.

Great New York Date: Combine a visit to the Noguchi Museum with a romantic late lunch or cocktails or an early dinner with a view at the Water's Edge (#165).

JACQUES MARCHAIS MUSEUM
OF TIBETAN ART

IF YOU TAKE the S74 BUS from the St. George Ferry Terminal in Staten Island, you reach the Jacques Marchais Museum by a ten-minute, quarter-mile walk uphill, the traditional approach to a Buddhist monastery. It is said that the trek enhances the sense of tranquillity you feel on entering the gate.

Within the walls of the museum is one of the largest collections of Tibetan art outside Tibet. Jacques Marchais is the professional name used by Jacqueline Klauber, a Staten Island resident and art dealer who had an abiding fascination for Tibet and who built the center to resemble a monastery. It is a serene place with lovely landscaped grounds, including a garden with paths dotted with prayer stones, wooden sculpture, and Buddhas that invite contemplation. Between two trees hangs a flag that Buddhists believe acts as a conduit of prayers to all living things. Inside the building are cases containing Tibetan, Chinese, Mongolian, and Nepalese art and artifacts, including thirteen 12-inch tall bronze figurines that Klauber found in her attic in Illinois when she was just a girl. Left by a long-dead relative who had been a sailor, in essence they were the genesis of the center.

On Sundays there is a performance or a talk, and in the fall a colorful harvest festival featuring Tibetan foods, calligraphy demonstrations, chants, and prayers. It is a peaceful haven for a walk or a talk and in fine weather a picnic, with a view of the Atlantic Highlands in New Jersey.

Jacques Marchais Museum of Tibetan Art, 338 Lighthouse Avenue, off Richmond Road, Lighthouse Hill, Staten Island. (718)987-3500. OPEN mid-April to mid-November Wednesday through Sunday 1 to 5 PM. At other times call for an appointment. Admission $3.

TEMPLE OF DENDUR

ALTHOUGH THE TEMPLE OF DENDUR is just a tiny aspect of the Metropolitan Museum of Art, it is a space that warrants a visit, even if you see no other part of the museum. Reconfigured at the Met to recall its original location when built by Emperor Augustin in 15 B.C. on the banks of the Nile at Dendur in Upper Egypt, it is the only complete Egyptian temple in the Western Hemisphere.

Enter the pronaos, or the open vestibule in front of the temple. This is the most decorated portion of the three-room temple, where only Roman and Egyptian dignitaries were allowed during ritual occasions. Visible from the pronaos is the offering room. Also visible is evidence that graffiti is an age-old problem.

The temple, housed in a dramatic, soaring glass pavilion reaching into Central Park, is a place of otherworldly beauty. It invites contemplation—and following that, toss a coin in the pool and make a wish.

Metropolitan Museum of Art, Fifth Avenue and 82nd Street. (212)535-7710. OPEN Sunday, Tuesday to Thursday 9:30 AM to 5:15 PM, Friday and Saturday until 8:45 PM. Suggested museum contribution $7.

P.S. For a truly memorable evening in the Temple attend one of the classical concerts featuring flutist Paula Robison playing Vivaldi, Bach, and Handel offered two evenings in mid-November and again in March. Call (212)570-3949 for specific dates and ticket prices.

WAVE HILL

23

WAVE HILL covers twenty-eight spectacular, peaceful acres of forest, gardens, and rolling meadows in the Riverdale section of the Bronx, overlooking the Hudson River. The estate, with its splendid Georgian mansion and horticultural garden, once home to Mark Twain, Theodore Roosevelt, and Arturo Toscanini, now belongs to the city. Only twenty minutes from midtown Manhattan, it's as far removed from it as Oz was from Kansas. It's a place to escape from the urban struggle, if only briefly.

This unspoiled stretch of country that miraculously endures within the city is a horticulturalist's haven, with more than 3,000 species of plants. Best of all it's a place where anyone can go and be calmed, a lush garden of delights for battered and sore urban spirits. There are woodland walks and classical music concerts on weekends, and wonderful performance-art events in summer, including dance on the lawn. Wander the seemingly casually planted grounds and your curiosity is rewarded—every plant is meticulously labeled. There are meadows to romp in, there are trellised walks with breathtaking views of the Hudson and the towering Palisades to relish, there are pine chairs on the expansive lawn in which to sit, read, or doze. And there is a small area for picnickers, so bring a box lunch or opt for the café with indoor and outdoor seating. What you choose to do when you get to Wave Hill is irrelevant—just get there.

Wave Hill, 675 West 252nd Street, Bronx. For information on daily happenings call (718)549-3200. OPEN Tuesday through Sunday 10 AM to 4:30 PM. Admission free weekdays, $4 weekends.

CONSERVATORY GARDEN

24

IN THE UPPER REACHES of Central Park, a pair of French wrought-iron gates lead you into a retreat within an oasis. In 1899 a complex of greenhouses stood on this site, hence the name. The garden's six acres were commissioned during the Depression as a WPA project; it's one of the most beguiling places in the city. The center garden is a perfectly manicured half-acre rectangle of green lawn. Just beyond is a raised semi-circular walkway, cooled by the covering of an iron-work pergola adorned with an ancient green and purple Chinese wisteria vine. It's an ideal vantage point from which to view the entire garden, a series of unfolding delights. Flanked by yew hedges and rows of flowering crab-apple trees, the north, or French, garden is a circle of tiered flower beds containing 20,000 pink and white tulips that make their spectacular appearance in spring. In the fall 5,000 colorful chrysanthemums dazzle the eye. In its center is the Untermeyer Fountain, with its three winsome bronze dancing nymphs and splashing water. Within the lushly planted south, or English, garden is the "secret garden," a natural enclosed space with a reflecting pool replete with water lilies and goldfish, where the air is perfumed by lilacs. In the pool is the Burnett Fountain, depicting the two children Mary and Dickon, from Frances Hodgson Burnett's *The Secret Garden*. An afternoon spent here is like paradise found.

Conservatory Garden is located on Fifth Avenue at the eastern edge of Central Park between West 103rd and West 106th Streets. The Central Park Conservancy trolley tour also visits the garden (see #43).

P.S. When you visit the Conservatory Garden (especially in June) don't be surprised if you see a bridal party or two; it's a favored setting for romantic wedding ceremonies and photo sessions.

THE WINTER GARDEN

25

SOARING 120 FEET and enclosing a stand of sixteen magnificent 45-foot California palms, the glass and steel Winter Garden is the visually spectacular centerpiece of the World Financial Center. New York's newest dramatic public space, it offers glorious music and dance performances year-round. But it's also a place to go for a hushed calm, especially in the evening when it's nearly deserted. There are chairs in which to lounge and gaze out the glass front toward the riverfront plaza and the Hudson River. It's also a spectacular spot to be—winter or summer—as the sun sets.

The Winter Garden is located in the World Financial Center, Battery Park City, on the Hudson River (West Street, just south of Vesey Street). (212)945-0505. OPEN daily 7 AM to 1 AM. Call for special events information.

Love and Tea in the Afternoon

. . . a tea ceremony is a communion of feeling, when good friends get together at the right moment, under the best conditions.

—THE BOOK OF TEA

*T*aking afternoon tea is a relatively recent addition to the New Yorker's calendar. It's an ideal transition from the rigors of the day to the pleasures of the evening, and an especially delightful way to fend off pretheater hunger when you plan to dine after the performance. And most of all it's a wonderfully intimate and luxurious way for two people to get acquainted, to savor a shared serenity out in, yet apart from, the rest of the world. No wonder afternoon tea has become so popular.

P.S. If you have to leave work a bit early in order to indulge in a romantic tête-à-tête over tea, so much the better.

Danal

IT'S AN OFFBEAT TEAROOM, this dark, cool-in-summer, cozy-in-winter café with one-of-a-kind antique tables and chairs. The formal tea, by reservation, is served at a leisurely pace Friday through Sunday. If you are feeling particularly indolent, you could reserve seating in one of the two over-stuffed sofas in front of a make-believe fire; a rainy afternoon makes this civilized repast even more welcome. Tea at Danal is accompanied by tasty tea sandwiches, like pear and Stilton cheese, ham and apricot preserve, and cucumber with herb butter, followed by a delectable scone, served with cream and home-made preserves, and then the finale, a choice of two delectable sweets—all served on Staffordshire china, for $12.

Danal, 90 East 10th Street between Third and Fourth Avenues. (212)982-6930. OPEN Wednesday through Sunday 9:30 AM to 10 PM. Afternoon tea is served Friday, Saturday, and Sunday 3:30 to 5:30 PM. American Express only.

P.S. Once you've found Danal for afternoon tea, I have no doubt you will return; it's that special. Try it for an early weekday morning continental breakfast (9:30 to noon) when the livin' is easy and you can get to work late—the two of you will practically have the place to yourselves. Or go for the delightful Sunday brunch of smoked salmon on buck-wheat blinis or French toast made with croissants (9:30 AM to 3 PM). In summer have breakfast or brunch in the tiny gravel-strewn rear courtyard. Come for a delicious soup and sandwich or salad lunch (noon to 3 PM) on a winter day when the café window is misted over and the literal and fig-urative warmth of the place envelops you as you enter. Or try it for dinner (6 to 10 PM) any time of year, when you'll feel as if you are at a rather casual but intimate dinner party to which you may bring your own wine. Yes, it's eccentric; yes, it's located in the East Village, a bit out of the way for most; but yes, it's well worth the trip.

ANGLERS & WRITERS

THIS CHARMINGLY SEDATE Greenwich Village café positively beckons you to enter, and when you do you're pleasantly rewarded — not to mention transported. Tackle baskets, stuffed mounted fish, and other accessories of the sport of fishing grace the walls, which are also lined with shelves of well-worn books. The antique oak and marble tables graced with vintage china and fresh flowers, and the mismatched chairs, all contribute to the feel of a country inn located somewhere west and north of the Rockies (a feeling engendered by the wide, open nature of the room, I suppose). Afternoon tea in winter with the setting sun breaking through the large windows facing west on Hudson Street is a special time to come here, either with someone or on your own to daydream or even to read a book — yours or one of theirs. Of course, tea for two moves this into a different category of romantic.

There is a wide selection of teas, and coffee too is yours for the asking. A slice of home-baked scone cake with cream and preserves, followed by a generous plate of savory open-faced tea sandwiches and salads, and then a blessedly small, sweet finish make up the prix-fixe tea ($12.50), and it's a treat.

Anglers & Writers, 420 Hudson Street at St. Luke's Place. (212)675-0810. OPEN Sunday through Thursday 9 AM to 11 PM, Friday and Saturday until midnight. Afternoon tea daily to 3 to 7 PM. No credit cards but personal checks are accepted.

P.S. Angler's & Writers is also an attractive, relatively inexpensive place in Greenwich Village to have a dinner of soup, sandwich or salad, and/or coffee and dessert while the two of you sit side by side on one of the couches. In the evening the room is even more inviting, with candlelight and quiet recorded jazz playing in the background. Dinner is served until 11 PM, a bit later on weekends.

FELISSIMO TEAROOM

28) ENSCONCED ON THE TOP FLOOR of a turn-of-the-century town house turned emporium (#112), the tearoom (with an adjacent art gallery) is a sedate nook with a Zen-like spareness where a delightful afternoon Haiku Tea is served. The prix-fixe tea costs $16 and consists of a finger-sandwich sampler, with scrumptious morsels such as rosemary pastry puff with goat cheese and caramelized onions, herb chicken with salsa on multigrain bread, followed by miniature scones, pastries, and organic osenbei cookies. Tea is chosen from a menu of herbal, green, and black teas. *Note:* Vegetarian sandwiches are available on request. Also, a wide selection of teas and attractive tea accessories and books are for sale.

Felissimo Tearoom, 10 West 56th Street. Top floor. (212)956-0082. OPEN Monday through Saturday 10:30 AM to 5:30 PM, Thursday until 7 PM. Tea is served 3:30 to 5:30 PM.

TEA AND SYMPATHY

THIS HOMEY, TERRIBLY BRITISH TEAROOM in a Greenwich Village storefront is no bigger than a bread box. Outfitted with cake stands, antique teapots, and tablecloths, it's a delightful spot for a "cuppa." The full tea for $10.95 includes finger sandwiches, scones with clotted cream and jam, cakes, and assorted biscuits.

Tea And Sympathy, 108 Greenwich Avenue between West 12th and West 13th Streets. (212)807-8329. Tea Monday through Friday 11:30 AM to 6 PM, Saturday and Sunday 1:30 to 6 PM. No credit cards.

T SALON

UNDER THE SoHo BRANCH of the Guggenheim Museum is this salon-café-boutique that is a veritable paean to tea. It's a stunning and tranquil (especially during the week) place to partake, with its sinuous seventy-five–foot long counter, Frank Gehry chairs, tapestry-upholstered banquettes, and antique and contemporary teapots and accessories.

The salon features over 200 kinds of tea and an interesting à-la-carte café menu, as well as a full bar. The copious "Proper Afternoon Tea," served every afternoon between 3:30 and 6 PM, starts with a blueberry walnut whole-wheat scone with crème fraiche and preserves, followed by a selection of sandwiches, including green tea chicken with peanut dressing, a smoked salmon triple decker with scallion and black pepper cream cheese and spicy sprouts, and red radishes and cucumbers with goat cheese on black olive bread. It ends with an Earl Grey chocolate almond torte, an apricot dipped in chocolate, and a fresh fruit tart. The cost is $22.50. The "New York Tea," served between 6 and 8 PM, starts with lemon shortbread and ends with a finale of house port or sherry; in between is a reprise of the above. The cost is $25.

Note: Be prepared to relax; service is snail-paced.

T Salon, 142 Mercer Street at Prince Street. (212)925-3700. OPEN Monday 10 AM to 10 PM, Tuesday and Wednesday 10 AM to 11 PM, Thursday and Friday 10 AM to midnight, Saturday 10 AM to 1 AM, Sunday 11:30 AM to 9 PM.

TEA DANCING — DIPPING AND SIPPING

Saturday Afternoon Tea Dances:
The most romantic way to have tea

31 SATURDAY AFTERNOON TEA DANCES, a once-a-month affair in the spacious, marble-floored lobby of an East Side building, are sponsored by Chartwell Booksellers and the New York Swing Society. The live dance music (featuring such elegant favorites as "Let's Fall in Love" and "Where or When") and the tea are free; sandwiches and pastries may be purchased at the Café Marguery, located in the lobby. There are singles and couples, dancers and listeners; it's an old-fashioned treat in an unexpected place.

Saturday Afternoon Tea Dances, Park Avenue Plaza, 55 East 52nd Street between Park and Madison Avenues. (212)308-0643. The third Saturday of the month, 3 to 6 PM. Free. Throughout the month of December "Holiday Tea at Three" takes place Monday through Saturday, when the tea dancing takes on a holiday glow. For more tea dancing, see the Book–Friends Café (#86).

The Palm Court

The Palm Court in the Plaza Hotel, opened in 1907, may be the last vestige of a genteel and elegant era long past. The still-gracious (though a bit overgilded) palm-bedecked enclave of the busy lobby continues to exude the romance of Old New York. It's a nostalgic choice for English tea, which here features scones, Devonshire cream and preserves, delectable open-faced sandwiches, petits fours, and a choice of dessert. Best of all it is accompanied by violin music. The Palm Court is a place without equal in this city, and whether you have tea or a luscious sweet and coffee, caviar and champagne, or Sunday brunch, you will be enchanted. Prix-fixe tea is $20.

The Palm Court, the Plaza Hotel, 768 Fifth Avenue at 58th Street. (212)759-3000. Afternoon tea Monday through Saturday 3:45 to 6 PM, Sunday to 6 PM. No reservations are taken for tea for two.

The Lowell

Tea at the lovely Lowell Hotel is offered in the secluded, hushed second floor Pembroke Room, amid Chinese urns, mahogany furniture, chintz and satin, far from the madding Madison Avenue crowd. Tea served with scones, finger sandwiches, fruit tart, and cookies is $21.50.

Lowell Hotel, 28 East 63rd Street. (212)838-1400. Afternoon tea daily 3:30 to 6:30 PM. Reservations are taken.

THE MAYFAIR HOTEL

TEA IN THE CENTRAL SUNKEN COURT of the Mayfair Hotel lobby, with its comfortably plush couches and armchairs, is an inviting affair, making you feel like a guest in a gracious private home. The full tea, for a prix fixe of $18, includes finger sandwiches, scones, and cookies with your choice of tea.

Mayfair Hotel, Park Avenue at East 65th Street. (212)288-0800. Afternoon tea daily 3 to 5:30 PM. Reservations are not taken unless you are a guest in the hotel (now there's an idea), but every effort is made to accommodate you.

THE PIERRE

TEA IS SERVED in the Pierre Hotel's extravagantly elegant yet tranquil Rotunda, resplendent in marble and murals. Overhead a painted blue ceiling with billowy white clouds soothes you as you partake in afternoon tea composed of tea sandwiches, scones, and pastries, all for a prix fixe of $19.50. Tables are discreetly positioned for privacy and the service is superb.

Pierre Hotel, Fifth Avenue at 61st Street. (212)838-8000. Afternoon tea daily 3 to 5:30 PM. Reservations are not taken for tea for two.

THE ST. REGIS

IN THE LOVELY ASTOR COURT of the gloriously refurbished St. Regis Hotel, the area between the lobby and the famed King Cole Bar, a relaxing afternoon tea is served accompanied by live harp music. The $23.50 prix-fixe tea consists of finger sandwiches, scones with jam and Devon cream, and tea pastries. Everything is made on the premises, including the jam.

St. Regis Hotel, 2 East 55th Street. (212)753-4500. Afternoon tea daily 2:30 to 5:30 PM.

THE WALDORF-ASTORIA

AFTERNOON TEA at the venerable Waldorf-Astoria Hotel is served in the relative calm of Peacock Alley, overlooking the restored art deco splendor of the main lobby, where piano music starts at 4 PM. The repast includes scones, finger sandwiches, and petits fours, all for $18.25.

Waldorf-Astoria Hotel, 301 Park Avenue at East 50th Street. (212)355-3000. Afternoon tea Monday through Saturday to 5 PM. Reservations are taken.

THE ROMANCE OF THE PAST

*N*ew York City is steeped in a rich history, and many beautiful and historic buildings miraculously have survived the centuries relatively unscathed. They are often off your beaten path, which makes them all the more romantic as destinations. So the next time you go in search of something special to do, become a time traveler without ever leaving New York City. Each of the places described in this chapter reveals an aspect of the city's past not easily gleaned in the rush of daily life. Each is endowed with beauty and legend, and even a ghostly tale or two.

ALICE AUSTEN HOUSE
("CLEAR COMFORT")

38

THE HANDSOMELY RESTORED HOUSE, parts of which date back to the seventeenth century, looks very much as it did more than a century ago. Standing on the easternmost point of Staten Island, it faces the stretch of water called the Narrows, between Long Island and Brooklyn. The panoramic view looking out to sea from the garden includes the Verrazano Bridge and the shimmering skyline of Manhattan in the distance.

Alice Austen moved to "Clear Comfort," the home of her well-to-do maternal grandparents, as an infant with her mother shortly after her father abandoned them. The extended-family household included a sea captain uncle, whose camera Alice began using at age ten. By age eighteen, with a camera of her own, she had already become an accomplished photographer. She photographed with a passion, creating an unmatched pictorial history of turn-of-the-century life in America, and especially on Staten Island, then a stylish summer retreat. She was deliberate in her recording, writing down dates, names, and places, plus the time of day, amount of light, lens used, and exposure time on the paper jacket of each glass-plate negative.

Alice remained at "Clear Comfort" until 1944 when, impoverished, she was evicted from her childhood home. Crippled and alone, she entered the Staten Island poorhouse. The Staten Island Historical Society managed to rescue 3,000 of Alice's glass-plate negatives; another 2,000 had been carted off by a used-furniture dealer, most likely to be incorporated into greenhouses after the emulsion was scraped off.

In 1952, a chance discovery of Austen's striking black-and-white photos finally led to recognition of her works and ultimately publication, allowing her to move to a private home for the elderly. Acclaim came to Alice Austen a scant few months before she died at age eighty-six.

The elegant old Victorian Gothic cottage, in sorry condition when it was vacated, was rescued from destruction and restored, using Alice's remarkable photographic record of her own home, and subsequently landmarked.

After visiting the house and seeing many of her photographs, sit on the gently sloping lawn that leads to the water's edge. Imagine what filled the eyes and camera lens of the privileged, imaginative, and gifted woman who lived here nearly all her life. It's a lovely place for a picnic.

Alice Austen House, 2 Hylan Boulevard, one block from Bay Street in the Rosebank section of Staten Island. (718)816-4506. Take the S51 bus from the ferry terminal to Hylan Boulevard. The house is open year-round (except major holidays) Thursday through Sunday 10 AM to 5 PM. The grounds are open until dusk daily. Suggested contribution $2.

P.S. In May and September the Alice Austen House is the site of a charming small-town outdoor antiques and collectibles fair. Throughout the year there are festivals, concerts, workshops, and demonstrations exploring Victorian customs.

MORRIS-JUMEL MANSION

IT APPEARS as if in a dream, an elegant pre-Revolutionary War mansion sitting high on a bluff majestically commanding the highest point in Manhattan, overlooking the Harlem River and the Bronx. The house, which reminds many people of *Gone with the Wind*'s "Tara," was built in 1765 as a summer residence by Colonel Roger Morris, who fought for the British in the Revolution. The house served as Washington's headquarters for a brief period during the war, but for most of the time between 1776 and 1783 the British were headquartered here. From then on the history of the house gets interesting.

After use for a time as a tavern, a wealthy French wine merchant, Stephen Jumel, bought the mansion in 1810 and lived here with his bride, Eliza Bowen. Mme. Jumel was a shrewd woman who had managed to have the purchase price of the house reduced because of rumors of ghosts. The illegitimate daughter of a prostitute, Eliza claimed that George Washington was her father, and had even tricked the young and wealthy Jumel into marrying her by pretending it was the last wish of a dying woman. She promptly "recovered" following the ceremony. Upon Jumel's death in 1832 the young widow took seventy-seven-year old Aaron Burr, the Vice President, as her husband. It is reported that she introduced herself around Paris as the Vice Queen of the United States. Following Burr's death, Eliza continued to live and entertain in her elegant mansion until her demise in 1865.

A visit to this glorious mansion-museum and its lovely garden offers a glimpse of one of the few intact remnants of Colonial America, as well as a peek into the life of an extravagant woman, whose elegant tastes are reflected in the graceful Georgian, Federal and French Empire furnishings on display in its fully restored rooms. By the way, rumors of the house being haunted—this time by the beautiful red-haired Eliza—persist to this day.

Morris-Jumel Mansion, 1765 Jumel Terrace at 160th Street and Edgecomb Avenue, Washington Heights. (212)923-8008. OPEN Tuesday through Sunday 10 AM to 4 PM. Admission $3.

P.S. If you visit the mansion in fine weather, plan to have a picnic in the lovely Colonial garden. During the Christmas season the house is handsomely decorated in period fashion.

OLD MERCHANT'S HOUSE

DATING FROM 1832, the five-story Old Merchant's House is often called the house that time forgot. Built as part of a row in what was then a fashionable neighborhood (now the hardscrabble East Village), it was purchased in

1835 by a wealthy hardware merchant, Seabury Tredwell. His daughter, Gertrude, lived in the house continuously until she died, a spinster, in 1933. She maintained the house "as Papa would have wanted it," with the furnishings and accessories the family had lived with over the decades. Upon her death the house and its contents were purchased and preserved by a cousin.

A visit to the Old Merchant's House is like stepping back in time—to the Age of Innocence, if you will. The Greek Revival parlors contain the Tredwells' original fine mahogany furniture. Upstairs are two large, high-ceilinged bed chambers; the front room was where Gertrude was born in 1840 and where she died, in the same canopied bed, at age ninety-three. In the closet her handsome gowns, bonnets, shawls, shoes, and gloves are all lovingly preserved.

It is said that Gertrude Tredwell became a recluse following the thwarting of a romance by her father and that the house is haunted by a ghostly presence in nineteenth-century dress—presumably young Gertrude. Shhhh! Don't say a word about it.

The Christmas season is an especially sentimental time to visit the Old Merchant's House, when the aroma of cider, cinnamon, and evergreens welcomes visitors for a nineteenth-century holiday party, including the traditional New Year's Day open house.

Old Merchant's House, 29 East Fourth Street between Lafayette Street and the Bowery. (212)777-1089. OPEN Sunday through Thursday 1 to 4 PM. Admission $3.

Great New York Date: Extend the feeling of another time and place by following up a Sunday afternoon visit to the Old Merchant's House with afternoon tea at nearby Danal (#26).

ST. PAUL'S CHAPEL AND CHURCHYARD

THERE ARE WHOLE TOWNS built around the fact (or sometimes fiction) that Washington slept there. In New York the place where the Father of Our Country regularly worshiped sits rather modestly amid the surrounding towers of finance and commerce.

Just a short stroll from the South Street Seaport and Wall Street, St. Paul's is Manhattan's sole remaining pre-Revolutionary War public building. It exists much as it did when it was built in 1766 as a rural church facing the Hudson River, which at the time flowed quite near the churchyard. Constructed to serve the "uptown" parishioners of Trinity Church, the walls of the Georgian-style structure are of stone quarried from the site; the tower is of brownstone. The interior is exceedingly handsome — some people might even call it pretty. The altar design is attributed to Pierre L'Enfant, the man who later planned what would become the nation's capital, Washington, D.C. The richly gilded pulpit boasts a featherlike crown at the top, one of the few royal symbols of the Colonial era to survive the Revolution. It, the Waterford crystal chandeliers, and the mellow color scheme of pink, blue, and cream exude a sumptuousness that is unexpected from the exterior.

The newly sworn-in President George Washington and his entire Congress came to worship here following the inauguration in 1776, and he continued to do so for the two years that New York served as the nation's capital. His pew in the north aisle is marked by a plaque.

Although Trinity Church's graveyard holds more famed remains, the simple churchyard of St. Paul's is said to be haunted by the headless ghost of an actor, George Frederick Cooke, whose head was said to have been severed from his dead body to pay his final doctor bills and was sometimes — some would say fittingly — used as a prop in stagings of *Hamlet*. The head eventually came to rest in Jefferson Medical College in Philadelphia. The ghost notwithstanding, the churchyard provides a pleasant place to sit and reflect. There are also musical programs in the sanctuary every Monday and Thursday at noon; they are peaceful affairs, seemingly far from the cacophony of Wall Street. But the most romantic day of the week to visit this part of town is on Sunday, when the area is nearly deserted.

St. Paul's Chapel and Churchyard, Broadway between Fulton and Vesey Streets. OPEN Sunday through Friday 9 AM to 3:30 PM. Call (212)602-0768 for information about musical programs.

P.S. Nearby, have a look at the architecture of a far different age. The Woolworth Building, at 233 Broadway, dubbed the Cathedral of Commerce when it was built in 1913, was then the world's tallest building. The Gothic tower, though now dwarfed by much of downtown, remains a splendid presence on the skyline, especially now that it's lighted in the evening. Have a look at the mosaic jewel of a lobby and try to find the caricature of the architect Cass Gilbert holding a model of the building, and of Woolworth himself counting his "fives and dimes." Or walk west on Vesey Street and you will find yourselves at the World Financial Center, with numerous dining, shopping, and water-gazing opportunities (see #25 The Winter Garden, #45 The Hudson River Esplanade, #46 South Cove Park, #142 The Hudson River Club).

EDGAR ALLAN POE COTTAGE

IN 1846 EDGAR ALLAN POE, then working in Manhattan as a magazine editor, moved with his consumptive wife, Virginia, to this rural wooden cottage, built in 1812 in what was then the village of Fordham. The Bronx air was thought to be more healthful than that of the more congested low-lying island boroughs. In spite of the move, Virginia died a year later, yet Poe decided to remain. It is reported that he enjoyed the conviviality of the neighborhood's taverns and the stimulation of the students attending nearby St. John's College (today Fordham University). While in residence Poe wrote "Annabel Lee" and "The Bells," which is said to have been inspired by the bells of the college. The brooding writer died in the little white clapboard cottage in 1849.

The cottage itself was moved across the street to its present location in a small park named for it. The Bronx Historical Society restored it to depict the time when this part of New York was rural. The simple cottage is a draw for mystery lovers and mystics, who come in search of Poe's presence.

Edgar Allan Poe Cottage, Poe Park, Grand Concourse at East Kingsbridge Road, the Bronx. (718)881-8900. OPEN Saturday 10 AM to 4 PM, Sunday 1 to 5 PM. Admission $2.

P.S. Poe lovers may want to continue the mood of the day with a visit to Woodlawn Cemetery. Founded in 1863, this gilded-age cemetery containing elaborate chapels and tombs is the final resting place of a varied group of luminaries, among them, Bat Masterson, Mayor Fiorello LaGuardia, the Woolworth family, Damon Runyon, and more recently, jazz legends Duke Ellington and Miles Davis. Obtain a map at the office and spend a fascinating afternoon wandering among yesterday's rich and famous.

Woodlawn Cemetery, Jerome and Bainbridge Avenues, the Bronx. (718)920-0500. OPEN daily 9 AM to 4:30 PM.

URBAN OASES AND MOVABLE FEASTS

A loaf of bread, a jug of wine and thou beneath a tree.
—THE RUBAIYAT

*P*icnic groves were a mainstay of city life at the turn of the century, with no less than seventeen in Upper Manhattan and the Bronx. Only beaches and amusement parks were thought to be more felicitous destinations for a day's outing. Today, not only are our choices of picnic venues far more plentiful, many are as unique as the city itself. As for gathering the picnic feast, nothing could be easier in New York with food shops every ten feet.

The effect on the mind and spirit of greenery and open spaces in New York cannot be overstated. The large parks provide opportunities not only to picnic but to boat and bike, walk and talk, listen to music, sunbathe, be solo, meditate, or meet new friends. The small so-called vest-pocket parks, by virtue of their location, provide opportunities for noontime trysts over take out and are gracious meeting places after work. They are sedate oases in a sea of people, cars, and commerce.

CENTRAL PARK

HOW'S THIS for a romantic notion? A handful of New York visionaries believed that green space and park lands were as important to the creation of a world-class city as sidewalks and elegant buildings. So they convinced the city fathers to set aside 843 acres of Manhattan Island, which in the mid-nineteenth century were occupied by a fetid swamp, a garbage dump, squatters' shanties, and a bone-boiling factory. Then they commissioned two more romantics, journalist and engineer Frederick Law Olmsted and designer Calvert Vaux, who then hired enough people to move 5 million cubic yards of stone and earth; lay 272 cubic yards of masonry (half of which was quarried within the park itself); build 30 bridges and arches, 11 overpasses, 6.5 miles of carriage drives, 58 miles of paths, 6 miles of perimeter walls; lay 95 miles of drainage and water pipes; and plant more than 500,000 trees, shrubs, and vines. Voila! an oasis of natural beauty (and you thought Mother Nature did all this).

You may come from somewhere with wide-open spaces, but think of Central Park as New Yorkers do—as nothing short of a miracle. If you haven't visited the park for a while, it's time to go back; no matter the season, there's a reason to visit. As for romance, it abounds, from the many places to picnic—some within view of Fifth Avenue, others as bucolic as the countryside—to sharing free Shakespeare and Metropolitan Opera under the stars, to rowing, biking, skating, sunbathing, and dining.

Literary Walk, from 67th to 70th Streets, leading to Bethesda Terrace and Fountain, is one of the most romantic lanes to stroll in the park. Two rows of stately American elms form a natural canopy above it, and busts of poets and writers line the sides. The walk is especially lovely in the fall when it is framed by a carpet of gold and red.

Graceful Bethesda Terrace at 72nd Street with its

beloved fountain, Angel of the Waters, is the architectural and emotional heart of the park, a classic gathering place reminiscent of the formal parks of Europe. It is perhaps the park's most photographed vista. Walk down the grand staircase and up along the east side of the lake to the Loeb Boathouse. In season dine alfresco at either the Tavern on the Green (#161) or the Boathouse Café (#133), or get some tasty takeout and stretch out on the rocks to the right of the boathouse for a picnic with a glorious vista of Central Park South. Or head east across the road and down the hill to Conservatory Water, where on Saturday mornings elaborate model yachts are raced by their owners, seafaring though terra-bound romantics. At the north end of the pond is the Alice in Wonderland statue, philanthropist George Delacorte's most enchanted contribution to the city, given as a memorial to his beloved first wife, Margarita, in a spot he called the finest in Central Park.

In the middle of the park, at 64th Street, is the Carousel, built in 1908 by Stein and Goldstein. It boasts the largest carousel horses in America. Don't be too embarrassed to take a whirl—you're never too old to reach for that gold ring.

Visit the polar bears, the most popular of the newly refurbished zoo's inhabitants, possibly because they are the largest. On a hot summer day, it's positively refreshing to watch 800-pound Gus and his playmate, 600-pound Lilly, frolic in the water. For more chills and thrills visit the Penguin House; their unceasing chatter as they cavort through the tundra is a hoot. In winter the two of you can warm up with a sojourn in the Temperate and Tropical Zones, a sultry, skylit rain forest.

In summer Wollman Skating Rink (#89) at 62nd Street becomes a miniature golf course as well as a place for daredevils to rollerblade. On the green north of the Sheep Meadow at West 69th Street, members of the New York

Lawn Bowling Club and nearby the New York Croquet Club take their respective sports very seriously. It makes for interesting viewing while you picnic.

The Dairy, at 65th Street, one of the most charming structures in the park, is a Hudson River Gothic-styled edifice built in 1870 to distribute fresh milk to the city's children. Its romantic loggia offers escape from the sun and a map to get your bearings (although the two of you might prefer to get lost). The building itself, now the park's visitors' center, contains a glass-enclosed twelve-foot model of Central Park.

A bit west of mid-park, at 79th Street, Belvedere Castle atop craggy Vista Rock seems to have sprung from the pages of a romantic novel. One half expects to see fair maidens and noble knights, and you just might if there's a production of Shakespeare in progress, at the Delacorte Theater just beneath the castle. Now a learning center during the day, the castle stands watch over Belvedere Lake. Up a seemingly endless trail of stone steps surrounded by shrubs, grasses, trees, and flowers, the vantage point lives up to its name — a beautiful view may be had from here, the park's highest point. It's particularly lovely to visit as the sun begins to set.

Rowing on Central Park Lake (#71) on a weekend can fall far short of romantic unless you get there at 10 AM when the boat concession opens and you are among only a handful of others. If biking is more to your taste, a bike rental concession is located behind the boathouse, where you can further togetherness by renting a bicycle built for two.

Yes, sheep really did graze in the park's Sheep Meadow at 67th Street until the 1930s (the shepherd lived in what is now the Tavern on the Green (#161). For a long while it was the site of all the free concerts and opera in the park, leaving it denuded and dusty. Now once more lush and green, it's the park's largest "quiet zone" — no radios, dogs, ball playing — just splendor in the grass.

From April through October, Monday through Friday, 10:30 AM, 1 PM
and 3 PM, the Central Park Conservancy's thirty-two-seat red trolley
leaves Grand Army Plaza at 60th Street and Fifth Avenue for a ten-
mile sweep through the park (adults $14). Call (212)397-3809 for
reservations. The ninety-minute in-depth tour goes to the most popular areas, such as the Carousel, the Dairy, the Chess and Checkers
House and the Mall, Bethesda Terrace, and Strawberry Fields, then up
north to the lesser-known Cascades and Harlem Meer, with stops for a
ramble along the Loch and a visit to Conservatory Garden (#24), the
park's only formal garden.

Bryant Park

Bryant Park is midtown Manhattan's only
public square, and its recent restoration has
turned it into a glorious haven that defies geography. The verdant lawn, the restored fountain,
the seasonal flowers, the perennial gardens, and
best of all the comfortable French park chairs (they're mov-
able, just like the ones in the Tuileries, so you can sit as close
to each other as possible) are just where you need them.
There are no "Keep Off the Grass" signs here; you are invited to picnic, to read, and to sunbathe. And now there's the
large albeit handsome Bryant Park Grill for indoor or out-
door-terrace dining and its more casual café offshoot with its
popular (with young singles) bar. Day or night, Bryant Park
is now mid-Manhattan's most delightful refuge.

Bryant Park, Sixth Avenue, West 40 to West 42 Streets at the rear of
the New York Public Library. For details on performances and events
call (212)983-4143. Also pick up half-price tickets to a music or dance
performance that evening at the booth on 42nd Street just east of Sixth
Avenue Tuesday through Sunday noon to 2 PM and 3 to 7 PM. For ticket availability call (212)382-2323. For dining reservations call Bryant
Park Grill, 25 West 40th Street. (212)840-6500.

Great New York Date: Every Monday night at dusk (approximately 9 pm) from June through September, Bryant Park is an uncommon place to watch classic films. The free alfresco film festival is almost as romantic as the old drive-ins (remember them?). So bring a blanket, a basket, a bottle, and your beau or stake out a strategic seat on the upstairs dining terrace of the Bryant Park Grill.

HUDSON RIVER ESPLANADE

ENTER THIS 1.2-MILE LINEAR PARK running along the perimeter of the residential section of Battery Park City and you are in a world apart. The magnificent riverfront walkway, lined with nostalgic lampposts and the familiar World's Fair benches facing expansive views of the Hudson River, is kissed by sea breezes. Along its interior perimeter are strung pocket parks, designed by sculptors and artists (don't miss Ned Smyth's Egyptian-inspired temple, "The Upper Room"), in which to pause or picnic. It's one of the most inviting public spaces in Manhattan, and it's the city's best new lovers' lane. Picnics are permitted but "no alcohol" is strictly enforced. And if it rains, duck into the soaring Winter Garden (#25) and have your picnic on the cascade of marble steps looking through massive windows to the broad, languid river. Or in the evening, after dinner at the Hudson River Club (#142) or in one of the area's other restaurants, amble from the North Cove Marina along the esplanade to the informal South Cove Park (#46).

SOUTH COVE PARK

WITH ITS SIGNATURE BLUE HARBOR LIGHTS, South Cove Park is positively otherworldly at twilight. Its secluded three acres with boulders, trees, flowering shrubs, and native beach grass, have a natural wildness akin to what the first settlers might have spied back in 1626, which is exactly how its creator, artist Mary Miss, intended for it to look. It's a profoundly evocative nook where the barriers between land and river are lowered—waves slap at wood pilings that extend above the water, a wooden jetty curves into the river, and a steel-and-wood footbridge crosses its curve. A spiraling black-steel observation tower behind the jetty, its shape subtly echoing the crown of the Statue of Liberty, offers a romantic outpost with a panoramic view of the mouth of the majestic Hudson River, the Statue of Liberty, Ellis Island, and Jersey City.

Walk through the Winter Garden in the World Financial Center to get to North Cove Marina. Turn left and walk along the esplanade to South Cove Park

---

P.S. Thusday evenings in July there are free concerts at South Cove. Call (212)267-9700 for details.

PROSPECT PARK

PROSPECT PARK in Brooklyn is approached through a gateway befitting its resplendence, Grand Army Plaza. The plaza's heroic centerpiece, the eighty-foot–tall neoclassical Soldiers' and Sailors' Memorial Arch, boasts an observation deck. At the top of the arch's 103 steps you can get a breathtaking overview of the park (as well as magnificent views of Brooklyn and Manhattan) and see clearly the master plan of Olmsted and Vaux, the park's designers.

Prospect Park's 526 acres in the heart of Brooklyn, designed between 1866 and 1874, is a sylvan retreat fashioned to conform to the natural contours of the landscape. With no through streets to mar the plan, Prospect boasts nature on a grand scale. Here you may meander or picnic in seventy-five–acre Long Meadow on the park's western edge, the longest continuous open space in any city park in America. Or you can hike through a rugged wooded area to the top of Lookout Hill or—perfect for lovers—rent a two-seater paddle boat (#72) and spend the day mingling with the swans on the spectacular sixty-acre Prospect Park Lake.

The area surrounding the beautifully restored terra-cotta Beaux Arts Boathouse, designed in 1905, is one of the loveliest spots anywhere to picnic. There are tables on the portico, and a small café is also here. Fine for spreading a blanket is the green adjacent to the Carousel, a wonderfully exuberant piece of whimsy built in 1912, with hand-carved horses, a giraffe, a lion, and reindeer, and an air-pumped Wurlitzer organ. It's next to the newly renovated zoo, now the Prospect Park Wildlife Center, which also rates a visit.

Prospect Park, between Flatbush, Ocean, and Parkside Avenues and Prospect Park Southwest and West. The IRT Lexington Avenue Subways 2 and 3 lines stop at Grand Army Plaza. Soldiers' and Sailors' Memorial Arch OPEN Saturday and Sunday from 11 AM to 4:30 PM during special exhibitions in the arch's Trophy Room; call the Prospect Park Events Line (718) 965-8999 for specific dates.

P.S. A visit to Prospect Park *must* include the splendor of the neighboring Brooklyn Botanic Garden. Romantic highlights of the fifty-acre garden include the Cranford Rose Garden, with its fragrant namesake flower in glorious bloom June and September; the small but lovely Shakespeare Garden, featuring flowers and shrubs mentioned in the Bard's works;

the heady Fragrance Garden, where the air is filled with the perfume of flowering plants; and, of course, the famed Cherry Esplanade, where in April and May Mother Nature puts on an extravagant show heralding the arrival of spring. Especially inviting is the Japanese Hill and Pond Garden, which beckons visitors into a serene setting of graceful stone bridges, Japanese lanterns, tall pine trees, symbolic rock formations, and a reflecting lake. Wandering the garden's paths, especially during the week in spring and fall, offers numerous peace- and beauty-filled moments to cherish.

Brooklyn Botanic Garden, 1000 Washington Avenue between Empire Boulevard and Eastern Parkway. (718)622-4433. Entry to the grounds is free; there is a parking fee.

RIVERSIDE PARK

48 DESIGNED AS A PLAYGROUND for Upper West Siders, this linear park was meant for strolling, and it's riverside proximity makes it a cool, refreshing spot for summer picnics. One of the most beautiful gardens in the city, the Garden People's Garden, a 6,000-square-foot communal garden, is between West 90th and 92nd Streets. Here a volunteer group of forty-five New Yorkers grow gardens for the pleasure of you and me. At 79th Street have a look at those few lucky romantics whose address is a houseboat. The 125-slip Boat Basin is the year-round home of those who have chosen both the city and the sea. How lucky can you get! Sunsets are great from this vantage point looking over to the craggy New Jersey Palisades.

Riverside Park, between Riverside Drive and the Hudson River, West 72nd to West 159th Streets.

DAMROSCH PARK

AT LINCOLN CENTER, between the Metropolitan Opera House and the New York State Theater, Damrosch Park is the perfect spot to picnic on a warm summer evening while listening to free summer concerts at the beautiful Guggenheim Bandshell, or even before attending the ballet or opera.

EMPIRE-FULTON FERRY STATE PARK

THIS BROOKLYN PARK with its sweeping views of Lower Manhattan north to midtown is a favorite of moviemakers and lovers. The park, three acres of open space in the shadow of the Brooklyn Bridge, with green lawn and benches facing the skyline, is a special spot for a picnic and a premier place to be at sunset. Then, after being dazzled by Mother Nature, head over to the River Café (#155), just south of the park, for a drink or dinner or to a concert at nearby Bargemusic (#9) or to the historic and charming streets of Brooklyn Heights and the Esplanade (#63).

Empire-Fulton Ferry State Park, New Dock Street at the East River, Brooklyn. (718)858-4708. OPEN in summer daily 10 AM to 8 PM, in winter 9 AM to 5 PM.

P.S. This park was chosen by *New York Press* in 1994 as the "Best Place for Outdoor Sex." (Just thought I'd mention it.)

CARL SCHURZ PARK

CARL SCHURZ PARK, with a tranquil promenade with benches overlooking the swirling waters of the East River below, would appear to be the private enclave of Upper East Siders. It's a "swell"-kept secret and a serene romantic spot at twilight.

Carl Schurz Park, East River between East 84th and East 90th Streets.

TUDOR CITY

OVERLOOKING THE EAST RIVER between East 40th and East 43rd Streets just east of bustling Second Avenue is a small residential oasis of quiet and green. In 1928 the river view contained slums and slaughterhouses so the buildings were constructed facing in, and this nearly private park was created. With its bird's-eye view of the United Nations, it's a charming place to walk after dining on the East Side of midtown.

Tudor City, between East 40th and East 43rd Streets between Second and First Avenues.

SUTTON PLACE PARK

AT EAST 57TH Street and Sutton Place is a little park long well known to lovers who come in the evening to gaze at each other, at the East River, and in the evening at the glamorously illuminated Queensboro Bridge. After having dinner in one of the area's restaurants, such as Café Nicholson (#136), it's a sweet, safe place to dawdle, as if in a Woody Allen movie.

Sutton Place Park, East 57th Street at the East River.

P.S. Another spot favored by lovers is at the end of East 55th Street.

PALEY PARK

IN THE HEART OF MANHATTAN, just steps from Fifth Avenue, is this tiny ivy-walled haven from the hurly-burly of midtown. The centerpiece of the courtyard is a twenty-foot-tall water wall, the city's first (1967), which dampens and cools the air in summer. There are chairs that can be moved, either to the sun or the shade of its seventeen locust trees, a snack bar for coffee in winter, and cool drinks in summer.

Paley Park, 3 East 53rd Street between Fifth and Madison Avenues.

P.S. Paley Park stands on the site of the famed old Stork Club.

GREENACRE PARK

A DISCREET SNACK BAR, a "brook," a joyous cascading waterfall, dense greenery—honey locust, azalea, Japanese holly, and rhododendron—sun, and shade. What more could anyone expect from a park tucked between granite walls in the shadow of fire escapes? Greenacre provides a lush oasis of cool, calm visual beauty. And it's in midtown! Meet here early for a picnic lunch in spring or summer, a hot drink in fall or early winter under the heated trellis, or a quiet moment after work before going out on the town.

Greenacre Park, East 51st Street between Second and Third Avenues. OPEN March through December.

THE FORD FOUNDATION

56

THE FORD FOUNDATION was the first New York City building to include an atrium — now ubiquitous — but this one with its tiered paths, towering greenery and wishing pool remains unique. Nothing could be more romantic in this part of town at midday than sitting dry and serene amid the lush plantings and trees when rain is pouring down outside.

Ford Foundation, East 42nd Street between First and Second Avenues. OPEN Monday through Friday 9 AM to 5 PM.

STARRY STARRY SUMMER NIGHTS

Summer's lease hath all too short a date.
—William Shakespeare

*S*ummer in the city can be a mixed blessing. There are, of course, heat and humidity, but there are also rare but unmatched gentle evenings when the air is clear and you can even see Venus (the planet, not the goddess). They are the sweet nights of summer when love is in the air and seeking pleasure outdoors is mandatory.

MIDSUMMER NIGHT SWING

THE MOST ENCHANTING ASPECT of a Midsummer Night Swing is the feeling that you're at a big dance in a small town, when in reality, of course, you're at a small dance in a big town. On these very special summer evenings the Fountain Plaza of Lincoln Center is turned into a dance floor under the stars with a live orchestra providing the beat. There is a charge to enter the dance area, or you can just join those in the crowd around the plaza, who are not shy about getting into the swing of things for free. The Fountain Bar is open for tall, cool, refreshing drinks between twirls, or you can opt for The Fountain Grill's Moonlight Dinner Package.

Midsummer Night Swing, Lincoln Center Plaza, Broadway and 65th Street. Midsmmer hot line (212)721-6500. Late June through late July, Wednesday through Saturday 8:15 PM to 11 PM. Entry fee is $8. To purchase multinight passes, call (212)721-6500. Call (212)874-7000 to reserve the Dinner Dance package ($25).

THE MUSEUM OF MODERN ART
SUMMERGARDEN

THE SCULPTURE GARDEN of the Museum of Modern Art remains one of New York's treasured open spaces, an inviting "room" with a splashing fountain, decorated with birch, weeping beech, begonias, and pansies, where you may enjoy free concerts beginning at 7:30 PM every Friday and Saturday evening in summer. Here is sophisticated summer romance on a shoestring.

The garden gates on 54th Street open at 6 PM when the best seats may be had; otherwise the two of you may have to cuddle on the ground. The Garden Café is also open for light refreshments, including wine and beer.

Abby Aldrich Rockefeller Sculpture Garden, 14 West 54th Street. (212)708-9491.

METROPOLITAN OPERA IN THE PARK

59 THERE ARE NO ELABORATE COSTUMES or towering sets used in the Metropolitan Opera's free summer performances in Central Park of "Tosca," "Don Giovanni," or any other of the operatic jewels in their trove. But what there is — a great lawn, trees, the skyline and the stars shining above — is pure metropolitan magic.

Metropolitan Opera in the Park, the Great Lawn Central Park (enter East or West 79th Streets). Concerts take place in June, performances start at 8 PM. The Met makes appearances in Prospect Park, Van Cortlandt Park, Cunningham Park, and Pelham Bay Park as well. Call (212)362-6000 for specific locations and dates.

NEW YORK PHILHARMONIC IN THE PARK

60 PRICELESS MUSIC presented free by the New York Philharmonic on the Great Lawn in Central Park is a summer tradition. It's a perfect time to picnic on caviar and champagne or cold chicken and iced beer, then as the light fades, lie back, close your eyes, and starting at 8 o'clock listen to one of the world's great orchestras play Dvorak, Copland,

Mozart, Tchaikovsky, and Verdi. The first concert of the season is always accompanied by a spirited fireworks display.

New York Philharmonic in the Park. For updated information call the Parks Hotline (212)875-5709. Other venues for the Philharmonic Concerts are Great Kills Park on Staten Island, Prospect Park in Brooklyn, and Cunningham Park in Queens.

FILM ALFRESCO

PERHAPS THE MOST ROMANTIC SPOT to see a movie in summer is in the outdoor café of the trendy Italian restaurant Le Madri. Movies are shown every Sunday evening in July and August in the tree-lined space behind the restaurant. You may get a table if you arrive early; otherwise there are seats arranged in rows. The à-la-carte café menu features pastas and other Italian fare; the films feature Marcello, Sophia, and other Italian fair. The café opens at 6 o'clock for drinks, food, and live jazz; the film starts at dusk (approximately 9 PM).

Le Madri Cinema Café, West 18th Street at Seventh Avenue. (212)727-8022. Admission $10.

See also Bryant Park (#44) for more alfresco cinema.

TAVERN ON THE GREEN GARDEN

THE LARGE OUTDOOR GARDEN of this exuberant restaurant is a spellbinding spot to dine and dance cheek to cheek to live music under the stars. Lighted by hundreds of Chinese silk lanterns and surrounded by hundreds of flowering plants and the lush greenery of Central Park, it's as romantic as an Astaire film (only the filmmakers used a Hollywood sound stage to re-create Central Park).

Tavern on the Green, Central Park West at West 67th Street. (212)873-3200. May through September dancing in the garden Tuesday through Thursday and Sunday 9 PM to 1 AM, Friday and Saturday till 2 AM.

P.S. For more romantic outdoor dining see American Festival Café (#128), Barolo (#131), The Boathouse Café (#133), The Cloister Café (#141), Lattanzi (#148), Le Refuge (#150), Provence (#153), The River Café (#155), Roettele A.G. (#156), The SeaGrill (#158), and The Water Club (#164).

BROOKLYN HEIGHTS ESPLANADE

THIS FIVE-BLOCK PROMENADE, as natives call it, features the heart-stopping view of the Manhattan skyline captured in so many films and books—the sight of which always seems to inspire couples to hug or kiss (not quite the way it is in Paris along the Seine, but pretty close). It's a perfect place for a stroll, especially on a sweet summer evening as the sun sets.

Brooklyn Heights Esplanade, from Remsen to Orange Streets, overlooking the East River.

Great Brooklyn Date: After sunset from the promenade, have dinner at
Bistro 36, 36 Joralemon Street at Columbia Place (718)596-2968, a con-
genial spot for hearty portions of good French bistro fare.

YE OLDE VILLAGE FAIR

IN A SEA OF SCHLOCK FAIRS that clog our
avenues and disrupt traffic every weekend in
summer there is a single solitary charming old-
fashioned street party that takes place on the
quintessential winding Greenwich Village
streets of Bedford, Barrow, and Commerce. If you are in
town the third Saturday in May, go late in the day to the outdoor café where you can listen to music and dance under the
stars while neighbors lean out their windows and enjoy the
view. You could swear it was 1940.

Ye Olde Village Fair, Bedford, Barrow, and Commerce Streets in
Greenwich Village. The third Saturday in May, noon to 10 PM.

CITY BOAT SHOWS

*W*ater is a soothing element. The sound and sight and feel of gently rippling water easily lull us into a pleasurable state. New York City is surrounded by water, and although by no stretch of the imagination are we either Venice or Paradise Island, there are a number of glorious opportunities to leave the city's canyons behind, if just for a few hours, and set sail.

In the nineteenth century the city's waterways were the highways of commerce and the route home for many. Now we take to the water for pleasure—and oh, what a pleasure it can be. So book passage, on yacht, yawl, ferry, rowboat, paddle boat, or gondola (so maybe we're a little Venetian). There's romance to be found on nautical nights and days out on these not-so-high seas.

WORLD YACHT

FOR YEARS TRAVELERS TO PARIS have cruised the Seine while having lunch or dinner, and for the last decade the same kind of scenic floating-dining experience has been available here, thanks to World Yacht. Each of the four yachts in the fleet is a room with a view, and even the most jaded New Yorkers have been seduced by the fanciful notion of the city skyline as a moving backdrop against which to dine and dance. There are upper and lower dining areas, both of which are enclosed by glass, and though there isn't a bad table in the house, the best place to sit is on the upper level, either at a window table or along the railing overlooking the dance floor.

Live music begins the moment of castoff and continues through the evening. Service is well paced, and as the sun sets you are put in the delicious bind of having to choose between gazing at the cityscape or dancing cheek to cheek — both are filled with tender possibilities. Dinner is better than you might expect, considering the view (but not considering the tab).

Don't miss the opportunity to go outside on deck after dinner, when the lights of the city are ablaze and the metropolis is at its most dazzling. In case you get lost in the stars, I'll let you know where you've been: The cruise slips down the Hudson River around the tip of Manhattan, under the Brooklyn Bridge, and a bit more northward. Then it makes a horseshoe turn and heads into the harbor for a close-up of the Statue of Liberty (even if you're kissing you'll know you're there when the orchestra glides into a patriotic medley), then back up the Hudson to the dock at Pier 81. I promise you won't be able to resist a languid sigh as you disembark after your three-hour cruise — this is as close to the *Love Boat* as you can get without leaving New York Harbor.

World Yacht, Pier 81, West 41st Street at the Hudson River. (212)630-8100. Reservations must be made in advance and charged to a major credit card, which must be shown when picking up boarding passes. Cruises depart year-round nightly at 7 PM. The cost is $62 Sunday through Friday, $75 Saturday. Prices do not include beverages or gratuity. A lower-priced alternative is to skip the dinner and opt for drinks, dancing, and the view from a seat on the outside upper or lower decks for a cost of $25. Gentlemen are required to wear jackets; jeans and sneakers are not permitted. Dinner patrons tend to dress up, which adds to the glitter. The yachts are climate controlled.

P.S. Unless you have a specific date in mind, listen to a weather forecast because the romantic quotient of this dinner is in direct proportion to how clear the evening is. Spring and fall are good times to go, when clear evenings are more abundant. Weekdays are less crowded than weekends, and special times to sail are Valentine's Day and New Year's Eve.

Dinner on a World Yacht is more expensive but decidedly more romantic than lunch or brunch, which are buffet style. If you can both escape the office for a long lunch and no one knows where either of you are, however, then the luncheon cruise can take on added luster.

HARBOR LIGHTS CRUISE

I ALWAYS RECOMMEND the three-hour Circle Line cruise that circumnavigates the island as a wonderful way for natives or visitors alike to acquaint themselves with *all* of Manhattan. Ah, but for the purpose of romance, the line's two-hour Harbor Lights Cruise, for which reservations are not necessary, is a delightful way to spend an evening on the water and offers an attractive, lower-priced, less formal, more spontaneous alternative to the World Yacht dinner cruise. The skyline view, after all, is the same on both. There is a bit of narration, which is blessedly brief, and then the two of you are on your own to gaze at the sun setting and the city turning on its lights. Cocktails, beer, soft drinks, and sandwiches are all available but to be assured of a more intimate evening bring a picnic on board.

The Harbor Lights Cruise sails from the Circle Line Plaza, Pier 83 at West 42nd Street and the Hudson River, from approximately late March to early May and all of October Saturday and Sunday only at 7 PM. From May through September sailing is daily at 7 PM. From late October to Christmas Eve the cruise is once again available weekends only, sailing at 5:30 PM. The fare is $18. For a complete daily schedule call (212)563-3200.

SUNSET COCKTAIL CRUISE

ANOTHER OPPORTUNITY to experience the beauty of the harbor and the skyline at night is provided by the Sunset Cocktail Cruise. This time you can set sail from the popular South Street Seaport, and it's a perfect transition from day to night. The boat cruises quite near the floodlit Statue of Liberty, and a tour guide describes points of interest.

Departing from Pier 16 at the South Street Seaport, the Sunset Cocktail Cruise sails from early May to October in time for sunset; call for exact times. The price is $18. There is a cash bar.

P.S. Primarily for younger in loves, from Memorial Day to Labor Day weekend there are Friday and Saturday evening music cruises, co-sponsored by New York area radio stations, also departing from Pier 16 at 7:30 and 10:30 PM, with two hours of cruising while dancing to the beat of pop music. The fare is $20.

PORT IMPERIAL FERRY

IT'S A TOO SHORT FIVE-MINUTE TRIP across the Hudson River to Weehawken, New Jersey, but timed for sunset on the outside deck on a warm evening the boat trip will put you in the mood for a romantic cocktail at the bar of Arthur's Landing, a short walk from the ferry pier. Facing the marina with a view of the midtown Manhattan skyline in the distance (would I tell you to leave New York for any other reason?), this is a spellbinding spot for either a pre- or posttheater cocktail in an uncommon setting.

Port Imperial Ferry, West 38th Street and 12th Avenue at the Hudson River. (800)533-3779. Ferry fare $4 each way. Arthur's Landing, at Port Imperial, Weehawken, NJ. (201)867-6060.

P.S. There is a free New York Waterway shuttle bus service to the ferry terminal on 12th Avenue along 57th, 50th, 42nd, and 34th Streets; call for details.

THE *PETREL*

NEXT TO OWNING YOUR OWN YACHT, sailing on this handsome seventy-foot yawl will do nicely—and you don't even have to leave Manhattan to do it! The *Petrel,* with its sleek teak and mahogany deck, was built in 1938, and no less a sailor than President John F. Kennedy manned the tiller when it belonged to the Coast Guard.

77

A variety of sails are available, but the one that makes the most of romantic possibilities for me is the spectacular two-hour sunset/moonlight outing from 7:30 to 9:30 PM. On a clear evening it's exhilarating to see and hear the huge sails unfurl and billow in the wind as the glittering towers of Lower Manhattan recede. Sailing in the city is a contradiction, but the rewards are particularly splendid when you disembark and there are no clogged highways to face.

The maximum number of passengers that can be accommodated is thirty-five, but the vessel is large enough for the two of you to carve out a private place on deck. There's a bar on board, and the setting is conducive to a picnic supper if you choose to bring one. Just remember to keep it simple, for those times when the crew has to "come about." A romantic hint for you big spenders: The *Petrel* is available for private charter.

The *Petrel* sails from the south end of Battery Park starting from early May through September. The price of the sunset/moonlight sail is $25. Reservations and advance payment are required. (212)825-1976.

P.S. As is always true at sea, the captain is, well, the captain, and his idea of good sailing weather may not be yours. If you don't consider choppy waters, sea spray, and snuggling in slickers a romantic lark, buy the rain insurance for an extra 25 percent of the ticket price. Or get around it by paying for one or several sails in advance and then call and book passage on a clear night.

GONDOLA RIDE

70

NOT SINCE THE 1890s has a Venetian gondola graced the waters of Central Park Lake. But now, thanks to the generosity of philanthropist and lover of Central Park Lucy Moses, romance is once again afloat on the lake. *The Daughter of*

Venice, a sleek, stately, black wooden gondola was bought in Venice and is now expertly navigated on the still waters of the lake by a Venetian-trained gondolier. After drinks or dinner at the Boathouse Café (#133) — or anywhere else for that matter — top off a romantic evening with a graceful glide on the lake Venetian style. Without a doubt, it's one of the most magical things you can do in public in Manhattan.

The *Daughter of Venice* is available at Loeb Boathouse (enter from Fifth Avenue and 72nd Street) (212)517-3623. The gondola, which seats up to six people, is available by reservation every evening, weather permitting, from April through October, weekdays 6 to 10 PM, weekends until 11 PM. The cost of this heavenly half hour is $30 and may be charged to a major credit card.

ROWBOATS IN CENTRAL PARK

71

CENTRAL PARK LAKE with its rock outcroppings, cattail tufts, steep banks, and graceful nineteenth-century Bow Bridge is the most evocative and romantic boating lake in any of the city's parks (especially during the week). The rowboats can accommodate up to five persons — but leave the others on shore and the two of you quickly row away from the bustling boathouse area into the private parts of the large lake. Let yourselves be inspired by the tranquil surroundings.

Rowboats may be rented at Loeb Boathouse at 74th Street (enter at Fifth Avenue and 72nd Street) spring through fall, Monday through Friday 9 AM to 6 PM, Saturday and Sunday until 6:30 PM. The cost is $7 for a minimum of one hour; a $20 deposit is required.

PADDLE BOATS IN PROSPECT PARK

IF LEG POWER is more your style, the two of you may pedal a two-seater paddle boat to your heart's content around the sixty-acre lake in Prospect Park, a picturesque setting of low banks, lily pads, and weeping willows.

Paddle boats may be rented spring through fall at the Wollman Rink (718)282-7789. Enter from either Prospect Drive or Lincoln Park Road, from spring through fall, Wednesday through Friday noon to 5 PM, Saturday and Sunday until 6 PM. The cost is $10 an hour, and a $10 deposit is required.

See also Staten Island Ferry (#6).

ISLAND
HOPPING

*N*ew York City is essentially an archipelago, a chain of islands in a network of waterways. The Bronx is the only one of the five boroughs connected to mainland America, with both Brooklyn and Queens a part of Long Island. Of the five boroughs, only Manhattan and Staten Island conspicuously wear their island's "apartness" as a badge.

Island hopping is an activity usually associated with the Caribbean, the Aegean, the Mediterranean. But right here in New York there are islands enough to explore, each having its own character and pleasures. Although it would be more romantic to sail away to an exotic tropical isle, get into the spirit of adventure and think of New York's islands as convenient, low-cost day trips—admittedly, some are more idyllic than others. Yet in the right state of mind a trip to any of them can carry the two of you far beyond geography.

CITY ISLAND

73

FOR THE TOWN-BOUND who are without either a car or the time to make a real escape, City Island is a bit of serendipity. Located in the Bronx, City Island is a salty old New England-style fishing village with a timeless quality: Victorian houses, picturesque cottages, church steeples, sailing vessels. The island itself is not very big, just a narrow slip of land, a mere mile and a half long. The main street, City Island Avenue, is easily walked, driven, or biked from end to end, and at its end you can gaze across Long Island Sound to Connecticut. To see more of the island's charm venture onto the verdant side streets and seek out some of the natives, "clamdiggers," to whom you will be mainlanders or outsiders—but don't worry they're friendly.

City Island is a boat lover's paradise with marinas, boatyards, and sail makers. The Land's End Sailing School offers three-day learn-to-sail weekends, and Tuesday to Friday the school entices city-bound couples with minivacations. It also rents sailboats to those who already know the ropes.

The island is also a seafood lover's delight and places to dine abound. For charm with your seafood enjoy a meal at the Lobster Box, 34 City Island Avenue, (718)885-1952, a prime purveyor of the crustacean for more than fifty years, located in a house built in 1812 with a lovely water view.

If you find that you just can't tear yourself away from City Island—or each other—indulge in a romantic impulse. Walk over to Le Refuge Inn at 620 City Island Avenue (718)222-5762, a charming French-owned Bed & Breakfast, for a room (they have eight, four of which, including one suite, have water views). The inn, a restored 19th-century sea captain's house, is fairy-tale like. The dining room, where some of the island's best fare is served for dinner (by reservation only), has a working fireplace. It is also the setting for a continental breakfast and on Sundays at noon for a captivating classical concert.

City Island is accessible by subway (IRT Lexington Ave 6 line to Pelham Bay Park, then the BX 29 bus to the end of the line). By car take the Triborough to the Bruckner (I-278) north; take exit 8B for Orchard Beach/City Island and bear right at the traffic light; then follow the signs to City Island. Finding a place to park is another story. Le Refuge Inn: single $60, double $75, suite with private bath $125.

P.S. The best time to go to City Island is in spring and fall, on a weekday if possible. The best way to arrive is by boat. That's because there is only one bridge heading onto the island, and it's usually choked with cars on summer weekends.

CONEY ISLAND

ONCE UPON A TIME, Brooklyn's Coney Island was a popular place for courting couples. The scenario: a ride on the roller-coaster where you just had to hold on to each other, next a gallop on one of the mechanical steeplechase horses, each of which held two, usually the woman in front and the man in back with his arms around her, and then on to the tunnel of love, for, well, you know. . . . Now the romance of Coney is that of a faded wonderland—located between the end of the subway line and the sea.

At the turn of the century people from around the world came to see, as one observer wrote, "an electric Eden." It's difficult now, amid the decay, to imagine such a world-renowned heyday. But somehow Coney Island survives and lures, surely more because of what it once was than what it now is. It's a wistful place, yet some of what it is can still thrill. The Cyclone, built in 1927, remains one of the scariest rollercoasters in the world. With six fan turns and nine drops, it's a long minute and fifty seconds, and it allows numerous opportunities for clutching your companion tightly. The Wonder Wheel, a 150-foot–tall circle of iron lattice built in 1920, continues to attract the unsuspecting, who think this is just another Ferris wheel, and rewards them with sweeping panoramic views. Young boys and girls still take a whirl on the B & B Carousel on Surf Avenue, but Astroland is the place to find hot new rides. The Parachute Jump, the 262-foot structure built for the 1939 World's Fair in Flushing Meadows, Queens, and then moved to Coney Island, though now a ghostly sentinel, was declared a New York City landmark in 1989, as was the Wonder Wheel.

If you're not going to the beach—as fine and wide a beach as can be found anywhere in this country—then walk the broad boardwalk and see a microcosm of the world. Visit the excellent New York Aquarium at Surf Avenue and West 8th Street. Its collection includes over 21,000 underwater specimens, among them a family of white beluga whales. A must, too, is a Nathan's hot dog, first sold at Stillwell and Surf Avenues by Nathan Handwerker in 1916 for a nickel. The hot dogs taste better in Coney Island than anywhere else (it must be the sea air). Don't miss the fried clams and the french fries, either. If you're more in the mood for good pasta, head over to Gargiulo's, the seventy-year-old restaurant at West 15th and Mermaid Avenue, where it is reported Al Capone worked as a dishwasher before he moved to Chicago.

Coney Island: Take the BMT Subway line B, D, F, M, N, or QB to the last stop, Stillwell Avenue-Coney Island.

P.S. If you head to Manhattan at day's end via the D or B line, sit in the first car and you will be treated to a breathtaking sunset as the train crosses the Manhattan Bridge.

LIBERTY ISLAND

75 THE TWENTY-MINUTE BOAT RIDE to the home of Lady Liberty provides lovely vistas, and an afternoon sojourn on the island with a picnic lunch promises a soothing interlude on any fine week day in early spring or late fall, when the crowds have departed and tranquility reigns. I presume that you have already visited the statue itself, taken the elevator to the top of the 154-foot pedestal, and then climbed the 171-step spiral staircase to the crown for the unforgettable crow's-eye view of New York. If you haven't, what are you waiting for, her two-hundredth birthday?

The Statue of Liberty-Ellis Island Ferry (212) 269-5255, departs year-round from the Battery in Lower Manhattan between 9:15 AM and 3:30 PM, till 4:30 PM weekends in summer. The cost is $7 to both Liberty and Ellis islands.

ELLIS ISLAND AND THE IMMIGRATION MUSEUM

76 THINK OF IT, choosing to leave everything you have known all your life, taking little if anything with you, and boarding a boat to cross an ocean not knowing what the future would hold. Surely these immigrants who entered Ellis Island between 1892 and 1954 were the ultimate romantics. They in essence made the country in which we live, and we are their heirs.

Imagine what the sight of the Statue of Liberty must have meant for those weary travelers, who then had to pass muster at the entry point to the land of dreams. Four out of ten Americans can trace their ancestry through Ellis Island, a fact that may make this excursion a personal one for you.

The island is a 27.5-acre parcel of land, the major portion of it landfill from the excavation for the New York City subway system. The first station to process immigrants was built here in 1892. Five years later the original wooden buildings were destroyed by fire. The present grand and ornate Beaux Arts building, topped by its distinctive four copper domes, was erected in 1900. For the 100 million people for whom this was the entry point it was no less than the Golden Door.

To reach the island today visitors take a boat from either the Battery in Manhattan or Liberty Park in New Jersey, thus arriving just as the immigrants did. You step off the ferry at the very same spot, and the view is virtually the same one they had. The imposing red brick and limestone building, still magnificent to our eyes, must have been astonishing to those just emerging from two weeks in steerage. Enter the restored baggage room filled with baskets, suitcases, and trunks brought from far away so long ago and you can almost feel the ghosts. The next step for the immigrants was up a staircase that was called the forty-second physical because doctors watched the ascending crowd for any signs of physical or mental abnormalities. Those who failed the test had their clothing marked in chalk and were separated out for probable return to their country; for them Ellis Island was the "isle of tears." The crowd then proceeded into the two-story registry room, the emotional heart of Ellis Island, the place where those who remained were processed. Today this sparse room with the original inspector's desk and benches encourages meditation and reflection.

At this point you can move on to see films with archival footage or listen to poignant recorded first-person tales of immigrant experiences in the tranquil oral history studio or go out to the American Immigrant Wall of Honor along the island's eastern shore. There, on copper sheeting against the seawall, with the bold skyline of Lower Manhattan in the distance, are inscribed the names of over 200,000 immigrants to America. Perhaps one of your forebears is among them.

Ellis Island is reached via the Statue of Liberty-Ellis Island Ferry (212) 269-5755, from the Battery in Lower Manhattan and stops first at Liberty Island. Ferries operate daily 9:15 AM to 3:30 PM, till 4:30 PM weekends in summer. The fare is $7.

P.S. To make this a more evocative visit try to avoid summer and school holidays.

GOVERNOR'S ISLAND

77

GOVERNOR'S ISLAND sits in New York Harbor just south of Manhattan's tip. The British set the island's 173 acres aside "for the benefit and accommodation of His Majesty's governors." Over its long history it has been the site of a sheep farm, a quarantine station, a racetrack, and a game preserve. Subsequently, it became best known as a fortification. In 1966 the U.S. Coast Guard inherited it from the U.S. Army, and will continue to have jurisdiction over the island until 1998. The secluded military preserve, reachable only by ferry, has the air of a serene small town. Some beautiful eighteenth- and nineteenth-century buildings remain on the island, including the Governor's House, a Georgian-style building dating from 1708; Quarters One, built in the 1830s; and Castle Williams, built in 1811.

The island, now a National Historic Landmark, hosts an open-house weekend every year in May during Fleet Week. It's a special time to enjoy this secluded island, to wander or to just relax on the wide green lawn with a picnic lunch and spectacular views of Manhattan.

For information on the Governor's Island Open House, call (212)668-3402.

P.S. If you miss the open house, there are frequent formal 2½-hour group walking tours (no picnics) of the island led by Big Onion Walking Tours, (212)439-1090.

ROOSEVELT ISLAND

78

THIS ISLAND in the East River directly across from the Upper East Side is now reachable by subway, but for the romantic heck of it do what I do—take the alpine-like red aerial tram from Second Avenue and East 59th Street for the four-minute ride across the river. It's a terrific New York experience for a little more than the cost of a subway token. The windows offer a 360-degree panorama of the city as you rise 246 feet above it. Then it's just a short walk to the riverside promenade for a picnic with a view of tugs and tankers. Afterward explore the relatively car-free island: You can't get lost—you're just a credit card's throw away from Bloomingdale's.

Once named Blackwell's Island, and then Welfare Island, Roosevelt Island has had a rather Dickensian past. By the turn of the century it was the site of a penitentiary, an almshouse, a workhouse, and a hospital for "incurables." Today it is a small-town island home to approximately 8,000 New Yorkers, only 300 yards from First Avenue.

The island, 2.5 miles long, has some grand but deteriorating landmarks; it also has no fewer than five parks, making it a perfect picnic venue. The haunting historic centerpiece of Octagon Park is the Octagon, the eight-sided tower with a staircase that spirals around a sixty-two–foot rotunda—all that remains of what was the New York Lunatic

Asylum, built in 1839. In addition to that relic, the park contains tennis courts, picnic and barbecue areas, and great views of the Empire State and Chrysler buildings. My personal favorite is Lighthouse Park, on the north edge of the island, a pretty serene spot with a restored James Renwick–designed 1872 lighthouse, where a few people fish and picnic; it too affords beautiful views of Manhattan.

Roosevelt Avenue Tram, Second Avenue between East 59th and East 60th Streets. The fare each way is $1.40. On the island buses cost 10¢. Also, the island may be reached via B and Q subway trains.

P.S. After your picnic, instead of exploring Roosevelt Island, you have the option of visiting several unusual cultural institutions in Queens via the Artlink bus, which departs from the tram station. The bus stops at the Isamu Noguchi Garden Museum (#20), Socrates Sculpture Park, and the American Museum of the Moving Image. The $8 round-trip bus fare includes museum admissions. Tickets may be bought at the tram station in Manhattan.

Great New York Lunch Date: If you work on the East Side in midtown, opt to spend your lunch hour on a balmy day having a picnic on Roosevelt Island; it's closer than Central Park.

STATEN ISLAND

79 ALTHOUGH THE VERRAZANO NARROWS BRIDGE provides an alternative, the Staten Island Ferry (#6) is still the most romantic way to approach Staten Island. St. George, where the ferry docks, has the historic distinction of being the place where the last shot of the American

90

Revolution was fired, by a disgruntled departing British grenadier (who was keeping track of these things?). The island, which was settled at the same time the Dutch came to Manhattan, is historically rich and with its wide expanses of green remains the most rustic and bucolic of the boroughs.

A visit to Richmondtown Restoration, Arthur Kills and Richmond Roads, (718)351-9414, provides a glimpse into how early Americans lived. Here, in a place originally called Cocclestown when it was founded by Dutch, French Walloon, and English settlers in 1685, century-old crafts and the simple arts of country living survive. Fourteen of approximately twenty-five historic buildings dating from 1690 to 1890 have been lovingly restored and are open for guided tours. In summer costumed interpreters and crafts-people re-create the atmosphere of a small, working, period village; potters, leatherworkers, carpenters, bakers, cooks, weavers, basket makers, tinsmiths, quilters, and needle-workers practice their skills. The restoration features special events such as quilting bees and lessons in nineteenth-century dances. In August there's an old-fashioned county fair; in October a celebration of the harvest on Old Home Day; and during the Christmas season candlelight tours of the restored buildings—and you can help trim the village tree and join the carolers. At any time you can feed the geese and ducks in the pond or spread a blanket under a tree and have a picnic.

From January to April, every Saturday night at 7:30 and 9 there are cozy tavern concerts in the period tavern, which is lighted by candles and warmed by a wood-burning stove. The two of you can sip wine, beer, or cider while listening to music inspired by the traditions of Staten Island. Before or after the concert you can dine or enjoy dessert and coffee at M. Bennett Refreshments, a restored nineteenth-century building adjacent to the tavern.

Also worth a visit, especially in summer, is the Snug Harbor Cultural Center, 1000 Richmond Terrace, (718)448-

2500. Overlooking New York Bay, Sailor's Snug Harbor was from 1833 until 1976 a self-contained retirement community for more than 1,000 "aged, decrepit, and worn-out sailors." Today, this gracious, historic eighty-three–acre parklike complex with lawns, meadows, and woods has been transformed into a spirited and delight-filled performing and visual arts center. It's a glorious place to picnic, especially next to Lower Pond, from spring to fall (the grounds are open from 8 AM to dusk at no charge). The site itself is something of an architectural primer, with twenty-six structures built between 1831 and 1918, ranging in style from Italianate to Beaux Arts to Victorian. The first building in the complex, erected in 1831, is the center of Greek Revival Row, considered to be among the finest examples of Greek Revival architecture in the country. In the Main Hall are changing exhibits of contemporary art, and concerts are given year-round in the Veterans Memorial Hall—intimate jazz, classical, chamber and folk music. Here too is the Staten Island Botanical Garden, where in summer you can hear concerts in the South Meadow and gaze at the superb greenhouse orchid display.

If a day in the country is the sole item on your romantic agenda, you need not go any farther: Staten Island is rugged and hilly, and to some it's the city's very own wild west. Clay Pit Pond State Park, in Charlestown, (718)967-1976, the first New York City state park preserve, is a bucolic 250-acre mix of swamps, bogs, ponds, sandy barrens, woodlands, and spring-fed streams.

The William T. Davis Wildlife Refuge, on Travis Avenue in New Springville, offers two major walking trails that wind through 260 acres of woodland and salt marshes on the island's western shore. The High Rock Park Conservation Center, 200 Nevada Avenue contains eighty-five hilly natural wooded acres laced with walking trails. Both are in the Staten Island Greenbelt, a contiguous expanse of approximately 2,500 acres in central Staten Island. (For information, call (718)677-2165.) Here the two of you can bird watch, hike, picnic in summer, and cross country ski in winter. No wonder Henry David Thoreau wrote of his adopted home, "The whole island is like a garden." And it's just a glorious twenty-five–minute ferry ride from what Staten Islanders tend to call "the city."

Staten Island Ferry, Whitehall Street, Battery Park (718)727-2508. Boats leave every half hour on weekdays, every hour on weekends, except between 11 AM and 7 PM. Car ferries leave every 30 minutes between 6 AM and 11 PM only.

P.S. If you are planning to stay for dinner, here are some suggestions. Aesop's Tables, 1233 Bay Street at Hylan Boulevard, Rosebank, is a pretty country-rustic restaurant in the vicinity of Alice Austen House (#38) with an eclectic menu and an outdoor patio. Biscotti, 293 New Dorp Lane, New Dorp, not far from the Jacques Marchais Museum of Tibetan Art (#21), serves delicious made-on-premises pastas, focaccia, and biscotti, as well as a grill menu in its delightful seasonal garden. The Marina Café, 154 Mansion Avenue near Hillside Terrace, (718)967-3077, serves good seafood from a glass-enclosed waterfront porch overlooking Great Kills Harbor. R.J. Tuggs, 1115 Richmond Terrace, between Bard and Snug Harbor (718)447-6369, near the Snug Harbor Cultural Center, serves fresh seafood chowder and ribs on a patio with a view of passing tugboats. Thursday evenings in summer, Caribbean music and food enhance that "island" feeling.

A Winter's Tale

*A*lthough the warmth of home and hearth are extremely seductive on short, gray winter days and long, dark winter nights, there are still ways to enjoy the romance of the city without waiting for Valentine's Day to provide the sentimental impetus to emerge. Winter walks punctuated with stops for hot chocolate, forays to a bar or café for a hot toddy, grog, or a bracing Irish coffee —and with any luck a warming fireside —or ice skating against the world's most sophisticated backdrops, are rewards for those who brave the cold.

If you simply can't bring yourselves to venture out and must resort to a video and take out, at the very least rent a movie with a romantic New York City setting (I've included a list), and order your meal from one of New York's fine dining establishments (almost any restaurant will deliver for a price). Or how about that most sybaritic of indoor pleasures, breakfast in bed? And if you find yourself home alone in front of the fire, curl up with that most romantic of New York tales, Jack Finney's "Time and Again."

See also LOVE AND TEA IN THE AFTERNOON.

TELEPHONE BAR AND GRILL

THE TELEPHONE BAR AND GRILL takes its inspiration from the traditional English pub, and the three fire-engine-red British telephone booths (they work) that form the bar's facade are your first clue. Inside, the long marble-topped bar is usually three deep with a mix of neighborhood oldtimers and newer comers. The attractive area opposite the bar is always filled with diners who find the contemporary American fare and traditional British specialties such as fish and chips and shepherd's pie satisfying. The dim lighting is conducive to romance, but *only* early in the evening before the noise precludes any verbal communication. That's the time to head for the cozy back-room lounge. Always inviting with sofas and candlelight, it's especially romantic in winter with the added glow of a fireplace. To promote those warm feelings order an Irish coffee or hot buttered rum, hot chocolate with a shot of Kahlua or hot spiced cider with or without rum. Every night but Friday and Saturday (when they serve dinner here) the two of you may linger in the lounge over drinks until the wee hours.

Telephone Bar and Grill, 149 Second Avenue between East 9th and East 10th Streets. (212)529-5000. OPEN daily 11:30 AM to 2 AM.

CHUMLEY'S

OPENED IN 1927, Chumley's is a classic New York bar. The unmarked and hard-to-find, nearly clandestine entrances (the second one is through a courtyard at 70 Barrow Street) on a narrow, out-of-the way Greenwich Village street testify to its Prohibition-era character, making it alluring to those of us who know about it and hope that no one else does. Once a writers' hangout where Fitzgerald, Dos Passos, and Dreiser felt welcome, Chumley's was where I spent my first evening as a published author (of the *I Love New York Guide*), but you don't have to be literary (or since there is no sign outside, even literate), to be seduced by this smoky old-time basement tavern. Winter ales, warming Irish coffee, and a fireplace ablaze are added incentives to seek out this particular winter bar.

Chumley's 86 Bedford Street between Grove and Barrow Streets, (212)675-4449. OPEN Sunday through Thursday 5 PM to midnight, Friday and Saturday until 1 AM.

P.S. A walk down the narrow residential side streets of far west Greenwich Village in the vicinity of Chumley's on a snowy night transports you through time—you half expect passersby to be wearing top hats and capes as the nineteenth-century town houses with their wrought-iron gates become the dominant feature on the landscape.

MOLLY'S

MOLLY'S IS ONE OF THE FEW SURVIVORS of the hundreds of Irish bars that once thrived in the shadow of the Third Avenue El, the elevated trains that plied their way uptown and downtown. It's very much a winter bar, a place to get cozy in front of the fireplace that is Molly's centerpiece. The old building was once a farmhouse, and copper plates and old iron skillets decorate the room. In addition to the blaze, Molly's has everything a comfortable, inviting tavern should have—friendly bartenders, a group of regulars, Guinness

97

and Bass ale on tap, bracing Irish coffee and even good food from a kitchen open until 11:30 PM.

Molly's, 287 Third Avenue between East 22nd and East 23rd Streets. (212)889-3361. OPEN Monday through Saturday 11:30 AM to 4 AM, Sunday noon to 4 AM.

OLD TOWN BAR

THE OLD TOWN BAR has remained stubbornly true to itself despite the fact that the area around it has become more and more trendy and in spite of its renown as the bar that was featured in the nightly opening of the "David Letterman Show" (pre-CBS). Vintage New York is the theme, and it's as authentic as the bar's original 1890s wood-paneled walls and 14-foot high tin ceilings. The Old Town Bar is a welcoming outpost on a cold Saturday afternoon when you've been to the Union Square Greenmarket (#10) and need some warmth, good brew, a burger, and fries.

Old Town Bar, 45 East 18th Street between Broadway and Park Avenue South. (212)473-8874. OPEN daily 11:30 to 12:30 AM.

BEEKMAN BAR AND BOOKS

THIS CLUBBY UPPER EAST SIDE book-lined boite cum library comforts with its plush seating, warming hearth, and opportunities to play chess, read, converse, or cuddle. Boutique fare and drinks are available until the wee hours, and on weekends live jazz is added to the mix. By way of warning or invitation, depending on your fancy, a cigar bar is a recent addition.

Beekman Bar and Books, 889 First Avenue between East 49th and East 50 Streets. (212)980-9314. OPEN Sunday through Thursday 4 PM to 2 AM, Friday and Saturday until 4 AM. Jacket required.

Hudson Bar and Books

85

HERE IS A TINY, ROMANTIC DRINKING ENCLAVE in Greenwich Village with rich cherry wood paneling, tartan upholstery, a polished copper-topped bar, ceiling fans, and a cozy U-shaped banquette for snuggling and easy listening to live jazz on Friday and Saturday nights, starting at 10 o'clock. A drinks list offers ports, champagnes, sherries, cognacs and the specialty, single-malt scotch. Nibbles include chicken and veal pâtés, smoked salmon, and caviar. But it's the books that make this, like Beekman Bar and Books (#84), appealing, especially when you want to get snug. It's a good casual first-date place.

Hudson Bar and Books, 636 Hudson Street between Horatio and Jane Streets. (212)229-2642. OPEN Monday through Thursday 4:30 PM to 2 AM, Friday and Saturday until 4 AM.

Book-Friends Cafe

86

THE MELDING OF BOOKS and food just seems natural—feed the body and the mind, and the spirit is sure to be warmed. The specialty of this charming once-upon-another-time bookstore is old and rare editions that span the period 1890 to 1940; the collection contains some splendid New York volumes. When you're done browsing the library shelves sit down at one of the tables in the back (number 18 is the most romantic) and have a tasty sandwich or salad or a complete afternoon tea. Ask about the café's frequent special events, some of which highlight the romance of old New York. Especially winning are their Friday evening tea dances to live music, where you may even find love at first sip.

Book-Friends Café, 16 West 18th Street between Fifth and Sixth Avenues. (212)255-7407. OPEN Monday through Thursday 11 AM to 8:30 PM, Friday until 11 PM, Saturday and Sunday noon to 6:30 PM.

YE WAVERLY INN

KEEP YE WAVERLY INN in mind on a cold winter night, especially if it's snowing, when being warm—both literally and figuratively—is paramount. The comfortable and simple early-American-accented 151-year-old town house (a restaurant since 1920) reminds one of a more amiable time. For me, dining here late in the evening is not only romantic, it's therapeutic. It boasts not one but two working fireplaces to warm you on the outside and simple traditional (read non-trendy) American fare, like pot pies, prime rib, and southern fried chicken, to take care of the inside. By culinary standards this is no One If By Land (#151), but prices are relatively modest—(consider the early-bird three-course dinner for $10.50—which can't help but fuel a budding romance no matter which one of you is paying.

Ye Waverly Inn, 16 Bank Street at Waverly Place. (212)929-4377. Lunch Monday through Saturday 11:30 AM to 3:30 PM. Dinner Monday

through Saturday 5 to 11:30 PM, Sunday 4:30 to 9 PM Sunday brunch
with live music noon to 3 PM.

P.S. Keep Ye Waverly Inn in mind in summer as well, when
its cobblestone rear garden is a charming choice for a cooling drink when you're out for an evening stroll in the Village.

ROCKEFELLER PLAZA ICE RINK

88

NOWHERE IN THE WORLD is there a more glamorous place to ice skate from October through
April than at Rockefeller Center, especially during the final evening session, which lasts until
midnight. And there may be no more romantic
skating in the world than under the stars and the watchful
gaze of a golden Prometheus.

Rockefeller Plaza Ice Rink, between Fifth and Sixth Avenues, West
49th to 50th Streets. (212)757-5730. Skate times daily 8:30 to 10 AM,
10:30 AM to noon, 12:20 to 2 PM, 2:30 to 4 PM, 4:30 to 6 PM, 6:30 to 8
PM, 8:30 to 10 PM, 10:30 PM to midnight.

Great New York Date: The American Festival Café at Rockefeller Center
(#128) offers a winning combination of a three-course dinner and skating
package for $24.95 (the $4 skate rental charge is extra). Dinner is available between 4 and 9 PM with skating between 6 and 10 PM.

WOLLMAN SKATING RINK

THIS IS THE SECOND MOST GLORIOUS PLACE to ice skate in the city, but Wollman has one thing going for it that Rockefeller Plaza does not have—especially in the Christmas season—and that's the absence of hordes of tourists, who are prone to avoid the park at night. And at dusk the Central Park South skyline from this vantage point makes New York look like a romantic Oz.

Wollman Rink, Central Park, East 63rd Street (enter from Fifth Avenue and East 60th Street). (212)517-4800. OPEN Monday 10 AM to 5 PM, Tuesday through Thursday 10 AM to 9:30 PM, Friday and Saturday 10 AM to 11 PM, Sunday noon to 9:30 PM.

CAFFE VIVALDI

CAFFE VIVALDI is a tranquil café, not unlike one you might find in Europe, situated on a quiet not-easy-to-find side street in Greenwich Village. There's a fireplace to warm you, classical music to lull you, and delicious pastries and cappuccino to tempt you.

Caffe Vivaldi, 32 Jones Street between Bleecker Street and Seventh Avenue South. (212)929-9384. OPEN daily 11 AM to 1 AM. No credit cards.

CAFE LA FORTUNA

91

CAFE LA FORTUNA is an ideal place to head after an Upper West Side dinner or an evening of opera, music, or ballet. Just a short stroll from Lincoln Center, Café La Fortuna, with opera memorabilia on the walls and music in the background, is reminiscent of the kind of place you might have found in Little Italy of yore. On a winter weekday afternoon it's a snug spot to linger over excellent espresso, cappuccino, latte macchiato, or hot chocolate and one another. As for the *dolci,* there are biscotti, zuppa inglese, tira misu, and more, from downtown's venerable Veniero's.

Café La Fortuna, 69 West 71 Street between Central Park West and Columbus Avenue. (212)724-5846. OPEN Monday through Thursday 12:30 PM to 12:30 AM, Friday and Saturday until 1 AM, Sunday noon to 12:30 AM. No credit cards.

P.S. In summer a hidden garden terrace opens in back. You may have to queue for a table, but it's worth it, especially if you order the delightfully refreshing iced cappuccino with a scoop of homemade gelato.

CAFFE REGGIO

92

CAFFE REGGIO, the wonderfully authentic and aromatic Old World Italian cafe, has been owned and operated by the same family since 1928. It is the quintessential Greenwich Village coffee house, the last of its breed, a remnant of bohemia before the world went technicolor, not to mention high tech. If only those cigarette smoke–stained walls could talk. There are soups and homemade focaccia, but almost everyone still comes just for the espresso, cappuccino, or hot chocolate and to linger and talk. It's a haven of warmth in winter, and a great

103

place for the two of you to dawdle into the wee hours of the morning over a nonalcoholic night cap.

Caffe Reggio, 119 MacDougal Street between West 3rd and Bleecker Streets. (212)475-9557. OPEN Sunday through Thursday 9 AM to 3 AM, Friday and Saturday 10 AM to 4 AM. No credit cards.

P.S. A sidewalk table in summer is a fine spot for coffee early in the morning before MacDougal Street awakens and the tourists descend.

LE GAMIN CAFE

93

I HAPPENED UPON LE GAMIN early on a freezing and windy Christmas Eve; it could not have looked more welcoming, nor more French. A tape of old French Christmas carols was playing, and I was immediately warmed by the atmosphere and then by the bracing hot grog. After a croque monsieur and a dessert crepe, the chef passed around a tray of just-made chocolate truffles in celebration of Christmas. I was charmed, and so will you be, provided you're a Francophile like me.

Le Gamin is the kind of place you might see on any Left Bank street corner, and it's a find for any time. Between meals it gets quiet, especially during the week, and you can linger over a large bowl of café au lait or hot chocolate, having a romantic tête-à-tête, or if alone reading *Paris Match* or *France Soir.* The staff is French, as is most of the clientele, so it helps if you don't mind cigarette smoke — Gauloises to boot.

Le Gamin Café, 50 MacDougal Street between West Houston and Prince Streets. (212)254-4678. OPEN daily 8 AM to 11 PM. No alcohol. No credit cards.

P.S. Keep Le Gamin in mind weekday mornings for *le petit déjeuner.* The cappuccino is wonderful and the croissants flaky; and for lunch there are sandwiches on warm croissants accompanied by a delicious salad.

BREAKFAST IN BED — CHEF FREDERIC'S YORK AVENUE PATISSERIE

94

YOUR BEDROOM may be the most romantic place in the city, and if, like mine, it has a fireplace, why would you ever want to leave it during winter? That's where Chef Federic comes in. With one day's notice and prepayment on a major credit card, he will prepare a breakfast feast for two from an unbelievable assortment of all he creates (with tender love and care) for breakfast/brunch on his café's premises. You have a choice of wonderfully flavored and filled brioches, croissants, danish, and muffins (including sugar free); or perhaps pâté, cheese, fruit, and some interesting bread; or the specialty, French toast or scrambled eggs with cheese and ham or mixed vegetables. All choices are served with cappuccino, coffee, or tea and fresh-squeezed juices, such as mixed berry or mandarin orange. Breakfast is delivered by taxi to your doorstep at a prearranged time. How you spend the rest of the day is up to you.

Chef Frederic's York Avenue Patisserie, 1431 York Avenue between East 75th and East 76th Streets. (212)628-5576. The cost of breakfast for two delivered anywhere in Manhattan is à la carte, plus one-way taxi fare. The service is available daily from 7 AM to "whenever."

P.S. If you wish, breakfast can be delivered to a special someone in a pretty gift-wrapped basket for $7.50 to $12 extra, depending upon the size and type of basket.

ROMANTIC MOVIES SET IN NEW YORK

These are all available at your local video store.

Breakfast at Tiffany's
West Side Story
Annie Hall
Portrait of Jennie
Manhattan
Hannah and Her Sisters
Someone to Watch Over Me
An Affair to Remember
Manhattan Murder Mystery
Barefoot in the Park

PAMPERING BODY AND SOUL

---

*N*ew York is arguably the shopping capital of the world and whatever you are looking for you can find it here, in triplicate, that's a given. But shopping in New York can be a passionate experience, not only for those who love to shop till they drop, but also for those who revel in unique environments where goods also happen to be purveyed. New York is blessed with many such emporiums where you can go and not necessarily buy anything to feel pleasured. These are the best places of all. What follows is a brief, highly subjective compendium of exceptional shops and services. They are engaging places to be considered when you are looking for something special for a special someone or if the two of you wish to delight in yet another aspect of this most romantic of cities.

TIFFANY & CO.

96

A JEWELRY STORE at the heart of a fable penned by a famed American writer just has to be a romantic place. Although you can't have breakfast at Tiffany's, if what you hunger for is silver or gold or glitters with diamonds or other precious stones, it's most assuredly being served up here. But don't think you must buy something to feel the romance of this famed emporium. There's nothing intimidating about Tiffany (well, perhaps most of the prices). The minute you walk into the store, a landmark at the corner of Fifth Avenue and 57th Street, you feel safe, just as Audrey Hepburn (a.k.a. Holly Golightly) did in the film of the Truman Capote story. You are free to browse to your heart's content, to revel in the riches displayed before you, and if you happen to be looking for a gift for that special someone, you've come to the right place.

The ultimate token of *amor* from Tiffany, of course, is a diamond engagement ring, in their signature six-pronged "Tiffany Setting," of course. But depending on your pocketbook, there are scores of other classic gifts of love, including a heart-shaped perfume flask and funnel in sterling silver, Paloma Picasso's "love and kisses" ring in sterling or in 18k gold. And could there be a more lasting measure of your love than Elsa Peretti's innovative albeit expensive "diamonds by the yard," although you may have to settle for the Italian designer's distinctive yet highly affordable sterling heart key ring. No matter what you buy, it will be wrapped in Tiffany's instantly recognizable robin's egg-blue box tied with a white silk ribbon.

Alas, if buying is not on your agenda at all, you could arrive at the store before it opens, as Hepburn does in the movie, and while breakfasting on coffee and danish, gaze at and delight in the wonderfully whimsical and engaging window displays.

Note: Adding to the legend of the store is the rumor that the most beautiful women in the world pass by this corner on any given day. Fellas, don't take my word for it. . . .

Tiffany & Co., 727 Fifth Avenue at 57th Street. (212)755-7800.

CASHMERE, CASHMERE

AH, THE FEEL OF IT. The softest fabric in the world, and also the costliest. Every item of apparel you can think of for a man or a woman is here in cashmere or cashmere blend, including tees, tights, and slippers. Could there be anything as sensuous as cuddling under a cashmere throw in front of the fire? Don't have a fireplace—then make believe. It's the least you can do for the Himalayan mountain goats and the herders who make the climb to gather the fleece by hand combing.

Cashmere, Cashmere, 840 Madison Avenue at East 69th Street. (212)988-5252 and 595 Madison Avenue at East 57th Street. (212)935-2522.

CASWELL MASSEY

CASWELL MASSEY, the oldest apothecary in America, boasts the world's largest collection of imported soaps, including one made from rainwater! Also in stock, Violète de Toulouse, the toilet water that aided in the seduction of

Napoleon, the fragrances used by two fascinating women, Garbo and Bernhardt, and boxes of Indian soaps bearing triptychs of Indian betrothal ceremonies (hint).

Caswell Massey, 518 Lexington Avenue at East 48th Street. (212)755-2254.

ECCE PANIS

GIVE US THIS DAY our daily bread—especially if it's from Ecce Panis. Here, amid lace curtains and old-world charm, bread baking is raised to a high art thanks to the Santo family, who own, among others, the Sign of the Dove restaurant (#159). Behold the bread—the light and dark sour dough; pepper brioche; Tuscan-style rosemary bread; sweet, savory or olive focaccia; and on Friday and Saturday only, no doubt to prevent addiction, the heavenly chocolate bread, a bread lover's aphrodisiac.

Ecce Panis, 1120 Third Avenue between East 65th and East 66th Streets. (212)535-2099. Also, 1260 Madison Avenue between East 90th and 91st Streets.

HENRI BENDEL

IF A STORE can be called sexy, this one qualifies. A mix of French and American design, Bendel's, which has the elegance of a private town house, incorporates the landmark Rizzoli and Coty buildings, the latter with its nearly lost, now

111

saved, Lalique windows. There are niches, half floors, landings, and little outposts galore, and you literally feel seduced into going up one more little staircase or around another intimate corner. Merchandise is temptingly displayed and I, for one, never leave Bendel's without buying lingerie. It's that kind of place.

Le Salon de Thé, in the second-floor atrium is a discreet spot for lunch, tea, or cappuccino and expresso with a delicious pastry, at a cozy table for two in front of those glorious etched Lalique windows. Extras include a concierge who can make reservations for restaurants and shows, and appointments to shop before and after regular store hours.

Henri Bendel, 712 Fifth Avenue between East 55th and East 56th Streets. (212)247-1100.

KATE'S PAPERIE

101

WHO WOULD HAVE THOUGHT paper could be so inviting, so versatile, so seductive? You'll want to buy a rice paper box for that little whatnot you bought him or her, some handmade paper for love notes to be sealed with wax and a seal (also purchased here), the way that lovers used to privatize their correspondence. What about a hand-bound leather journal to record your most private thoughts, or to hold the love poems you will surely write some day? There are photo albums, storage boxes, diaries, pens, inks, and picture frames, all unique and desirable, but mostly there's paper, for wrapping, for writing, for printmaking, for creating, PAPER, paper, everywhere—handmade, marbled, papyrus, lace, rice—over 8,000 varieties of sheet paper, all in a gorgeous, spacious high-ceilinged store. There's no other place like Kate's Paperie (except her other outpost in Greenwich Village).

Kate's Paperie, 561 Broadway between Prince and Spring Streets. (212)941-9816. Also, 8 West 13th Street between Fifth and Sixth Avenues. (212)633-0570.

LA MAISON DU CHOCOLAT

THIS IS WHERE TO GO when you want to bring someone the most irresistible sweet morsels ever created—champagne truffles. The only way to make the gesture more romantic is for both of you to go to the master Parisian chocolatier Robert Lixe's original shop—in Paris. Other treats include Bacchus (you know about that fellow), concocted of rum, raisins, and dark chocolate, and incredible chocolate-covered marrons glacés. Expensive, yes. Worth it? *Sans doute.*

La Maison Du Chocolat, 25 East 73rd Street between Fifth and Madison Avenues. (212)744-7117.

ONLY HEARTS

FOR SHAMELESS ROMANTICS who gotta have heart, this is where to find it on everything from clothing, to collectibles, to jewelry, to stationery. But best of all is their fine line of sexy, sensous, silky lingerie.

Only Hearts, 386 Columbus Avenue between West 79th and West 78th Streets. (212)724-5608.

POLO/RALPH LAUREN

THE BARONIAL RHINELANDER MANSION built in the 1890s for Mrs. Gertrude Rhinelander Waldo, who mysteriously never moved in when it was completed, is now the Palazzo Polo with Persian carpets, polished armoires, leather arm-chairs, ancestral portraits, and little bedrooms where you just ache to wake (wouldn't it be lovely to be left behind after closing?). Go up the stunning staircase leading to the second floor, gaze at the ornately swirling ceiling, at the carpets and chandeliers, and don't miss the gorgeous rest rooms. It's all the perfect romantic setting for Ralph Lauren's well-bred classic version of the way we were and, if he has his way, will be once again.

Polo/Ralph Lauren, 867 Madison Avenue at East 72nd Street. (212)606-2100.

RITA FORD MUSIC BOXES

TO SERENADE YOUR SWEETHEART, pick out a magnificent antique or contemporary music box with one of their tunes, or surely among literal-ly hundreds of choices you will find one that plays "your" song.

Rita Ford Music Boxes, 19 East 65th Street. (212)535-6717.

RENNY FLORIST

RENNY, located in a nineteenth-century East Side town house, is a flower shop masquerading as an enchanted garden. Orchids are a specialty, and one shouldn't be surprised that they thrive in this rarified environment. Though the shop operates mainly as a designer for a discriminating social and corporate clientele, a floral bouquet may be had for at least $45 (the minimum). It's sure to have that unmistakable Renny signature—a lush exquisite arrangement of nature's bounty with a master's touch.

Renny Florist, 27 East 64th Street between Lexington and Third Avenues. (212)288-7000.

SHERRY-LEHMANN

SHERRY-LEHMANN is a handsome place to browse for that perfect "jug of wine" for your picnic or a magnum of champagne for something even more special. The staff is knowledgeable and whatever the occasion, you will find the right alcoholic accompaniment here.

Sherry-Lehmann, 679 Madison Avenue between East 61st and East 62nd Streets. (212)838-7500.

GOLDBERG'S PIZZERIA

GOLDBERG'S PIZZERIA offers a novel alterative to a box of chocolates. If you've gotta have heart and eat as well, opt for a heart-shaped deep-dish pizza for two in any combination they usually feature, served in a bright heart-shaped red aluminum pan. The choice of toppings includes mushrooms, broccoli, a variety of cheeses, fresh tomatoes, or pineapple (on the Hawaiian). The good news is that this high-cholesterol (that's the bad news) token of your affection is available without notice any time—not just on that one day that Hallmark says is for love.

Goldberg's Pizzeria, 996 Second Avenue between East 52nd and East 53rd Streets. (212)593-2172.

THE PARIS APARTMENT

THE PARIS APARTMENT is a sentimental little nook crammed full of sweet old things for boudoir and bath. It is the complete antithesis of Ikea, in both scale and stock. The evocative window display and the constantly changing inventory of small accessories and bibelots are enticing, especially for those of us who are convinced we once lived in Paris in another life. Many are drawn to the small-scale furnishings—side tables, boudoir chairs, even chaise lounges—perfect for the reality of a small New York apartment. The Paris Apartment delights, it also amazes with the sheer quantity of merchandise so attractively purveyed in so small a space.

Note: Prices are not as low as you might think — or like.

The Paris Apartment, 328 East 9th Street between First and Second Avenues. (212)780-0232.

P.S. Like most of downtown, the East Village tends to sleep late — actually, it's more than likely unconscious. So if you are wandering around the area early and are hungry, have one of the justly famous low-cost hearty breakfasts at unromantic but homey Veselka at Second Avenue and East 9th Street.

LITTLE RICKIE

THIS EAST VILLAGE STORE is notable for its stock of whimsical, nonsensical, nostalgic, irreverent, and in some cases, truly shocking whatnots. It's a toy store for adults who've never grown up, and with prices that range from 10 cents (to a thousand dollars) you can have fun without doing much damage. But best of all, Little Rickie is also home to the last black-and-white-photo booth in the city. Four shots for a dollar against a choice of backdrops such as forties Hawaiian. It's a giggle.

Little Rickie, 49½ First Avenue at East 3rd Street. (212)505-6467.

ANNEX ANTIQUES MARKET

THIS IS THE CLOSEST NEW YORK comes to matching the famed Marché aux Puces in Paris and it's worth a browse if the two of you have any interest in the detritus of Western civilization. Much of what you'll see will give you something to chuckle over, but serious collectors can find true treasures among the trash. The romance of the past can be seductive for some, who come here weekly to cull antique clothing, jewelry, and other accessories, then turn up wearing it all the following Sunday. The people-watching here can also be enticing. Catherine Deneuve, Brooke Shields, Sylvia Miles, not to mention some of the hottest young fashion designers looking for inspiration, are often seen browsing the stalls. Best in April.

Annex Antiques Market, Sixth Avenue at West 26th Street. (212)243-5343. Every Saturday and Sunday year-round 9 AM to 6 PM.

P.S. If the two of you are collectors or are trying to furnish an apartment with a unique point of view, you will be happy to know that this area of Chelsea has become an antiques and collectibles mecca with no less than three outside and four indoor markets within one block of one another. So be prepared to spend the day. If you get hungry, or in winter want to warm up, head to Lox Around the Clock, 676 Sixth Avenue at West 21st Street, (212)691-3535, for bagels and lox, that New York Sunday tradition. Sit outside if the weather is fine. For more contemporary home accessories stop in at Bed, Bath and Beyond, 620 Sixth Avenue at West 18th Street, (212)255-3550, the housewares-and-more store that's an ode to the nineties' nesting instinct. If your relationship hasn't progressed that far yet, go directly to the Barnes & Noble super-store, 675 Sixth Avenue at West 22nd Street, (212) 727-1227, and search out that perfect book to move it along. Alone? Go to the bookstore's café for a cup of Starbucks coffee and a sweet, and perhaps you won't stay that way for long.

FELISSIMO

FELISSIMO may be the most seductively serene shop in the city. It's the perfect place to look for a unique, and in many instances handcrafted, present in a wide price range. Forgo the elevator, ascend the gently sweeping staircase, and wander from floor to floor of the beautiful, neoclassical turn-of-the-century limestone town house of this Japanese retailer. You will be captivated by the small but exquisite selection of natural fiber clothing for men and women, as well as jewelry, home accessories, linens, scents and soaps, books, handmade cards, and other artful creations. Prices range from two dollars to thousands, and no matter what its cost, they graciously and beautifully gift wrap your purchase. On the top floor is an art gallery and a tea room for lunch, coffee, or afternoon tea (see #28).

Felissimo, 10 West 56th Street. (212)247-5656.

P.S. Felissimo's bridal registry offers uncommon gifts for the home.

THE PENINSULA SPA

THIS TRILEVEL ROOFTOP URBAN SPA offers relaxation and fitness with panoramic city views. It's a sybarite's delight and the most romantic health spa in town by virtue of its location on the twenty-first floor overlooking Fifth

Avenue. There's a spacious wraparound sun deck, as well as a glass-enclosed 45-foot swimming pool. The Spa Splurge includes lunch poolside with the midtown Manhattan skyline as backdrop, then a European deep cleansing facial for her or a European skin care treatment for him, followed by a Swedish or Shiatsu massage. Sauna, steam, and whirlpool are included, as well as use of the fitness facilities, swimming pool, locker room, robe, slippers, and personal-care amenities. The Executive Relaxation Day includes all of the above without lunch, or you could put together your own package of three treatments. It makes a great gift—to yourself or someone you love as much.

Peninsula Spa, Peninsula New York Hotel, 700 Fifth Avenue at 55th Street, 21st floor. (212)903-3910. Spa Splurge $297.75, including tax and gratuities; Executive Relaxation Day $226.10.

PUBLIC DECLARATIONS OF LOVE

SKYWRITE IT

IF YOU HAVE A YEN to write "I Love You" a thousand feet tall and eight miles long across the sky—and you have $1,000 to pay for it—call Mort Arken at Skytypers East (718)507-5220. Your message of up to thirty letters will be visible in an area of 400 square miles for thirty minutes.

P.S. Yoko Ono did this for John Lennon's birthday in 1980—in fact, I saw it sprawled across the sky!

FRONT PAGE OF *The New York Times*

WANT TO MAKE YOUR LOVE front-page news (and you're neither famous nor infamous?) For $330 a line (two-line minimum, six-line maximum) your declaration of love or proposal is positioned at the bottom of the first page of the main section of *The New York Times* Monday through Saturday (for the Sunday edition, add $100 a line). Call (212)556-7135 or fax your copy to (212)556-7074.

New York at Night: Isn't It Romantic?

A night out on the town is usually reserved for special occasions, in part because in New York such an evening requires planning. But any evening out can be turned into a memorable one with a bit of creativity. For example, instead of having drinks where you plan to dine, start out at a stylish boîte where the atmoshpere turns having a cocktail into a liaison. Attending a performance at the Metropolitan Opera House? Intermission becomes a romantic tryst when your preordered champagne and strawberries await your arrival at the Grand Tier Restaurant. Or follow even a modest dinner with a night-cap in an impressive setting, preferably a room with a view unabashedly designed to encourage romance.

"Everything old is new again" is a phrase worth repeating when it comes to what makes an evening out in New York a romantic memory. Champagne, cocktails, candle-light, and conversation against the backdrop of one of the world's most dazzling cities can make even the most jaded New Yorker turn tender. And where else in the world are the songs of George Gershwin, Richard Rodgers, and Cole Porter preformed nightly as if they were written just yesterday? "I happen to like New York," goes the Cole Porter tune—after a night out on this town you'll appreciate its tongue-in-check understatement all the more.

BEMELMANS BAR

LOCATED IN THE CARLYLE HOTEL, Bemelmans looks and feels as if it sprang from the paintbox of a Hollywood set designer who was told, "I want something very New York, understated yet sophisticated, snug yet worldly, where both Fred Astaire and Madeline would feel comfortable." Madeline, the charming children's book character who resides in Paris, comes to mind because much of what's special about this bar did emerge from a palette—that of Austrian émigré Ludwig Bemelmans. In 1947 canvas was applied to the walls and Bemelmans, who lived in the hotel, applied to the canvas his own whimsical view of New York. There are Edwardian rabbits having cocktails, police chasing art thieves through the Metropolitan Museum, and dozens of smock-clad Madelines in the charge of a nun. Bemelmans Bar is of another time, but it's hard to say when, so in a way it is also timeless. Cocktails never went out of fashion here; neither did the kind of piano music you can listen to and still hear yourself and your companion talk. It's the perfect Upper East Side spot for a rendezvous after work, or a nightcap.

Bemelmans Bar, Carlyle Hotel, 35 East 76th Street. (212)744-1600. OPEN Monday through Saturday 11 AM to 2 AM, Sunday noon to 1 AM. Music every night but Sunday at 10 PM. Cover charge $5.

TEMPLE BAR

DOWNTOWN'S RETRO GLAMOROUS EVOCATION of a swank uptown cocktail bar resides behind a nondescript facade in NoHo. Intimate and dark, early in the evening early in the week before going on to dinner in the village or SoHo, this is an inviting place to have the Temple Bar's signature drink, a well-concocted martini served in an oversized glass. The bar's other most popular libation is champagne, so you can tell where this crowd is coming from—or going to. Caviar, bruschetta, oysters on the half shell, goat cheese, roasted tomato pizza, and other boutique fare round out this stylish boîte experience.

Temple Bar, 332 Lafayette Street between Bleecker and East Houston Streets. (212)925-4242. OPEN Monday through Thursday 5 PM to 1 AM, Friday and Saturday 5 PM to 2 AM, Sunday 7 PM to 1 AM. No reservations are taken.

THE OAK BAR

117) THIS COULD BE THE QUINTESSENTIAL New York bar—provided you are well heeled (or your date is). But look around at all that wood, the leather banquettes, the Central Park vista filling oversized windows, the Edward Shinn murals. Could there be a more darkly handsome place for the comfort of a cosmopolitan cocktail? The Oak Bar was designed to be a gentlemen's bar, and there was a time when women were not allowed until after 3 PM. Waiters with bow ties and white dinner jackets look as if they've been there forever, and some of them have. Places where you can get history with your liquor are fast becoming extinct, so make it a point to rendezvous before dinner at the Oak Bar, where George M. Cohan, John Barrymore, Charlie Chaplin, and Marilyn Monroe, to name a few, all imbibed before you.

Oak Bar, Plaza Hotel, 58th Street at Fifth Avenue. (212)546-5320. OPEN 7 days 11 AM to 2 AM. Food is available until midnight.

TENTH STREET LOUNGE

THIS DARK, TRENDY DOWNTOWN spot with comfy sofas, oversized wooden chairs, and altar candles around the periphery of the room can actually be intimate and romantic early in the evening for a cocktail or espresso when its shuttered facade is rolled open but before the velvet rope goes up and the crowds and noise arrive.

Tenth Street Lounge, 212 East 10th Street between First and Second Avenues. (212)473-5252. OPEN daily 4 PM to 4 AM. American Express only.

TOP OF THE SIXES

TOWERING THIRTY-NINE STORIES above Fifth Avenue, the Top of the Sixes, though not a fine dining destination, is one of the classiest venues for a sunset drink this town has to offer. The view from the bar area is north, and you can see straight up Fifth Avenue to Central Park; it's also a good vantage point from which to see the Chippendale topper on the Sony (formerly AT&T) Building. Best of all for such impressive surroundings there is neither a cover nor a minimum charge, and nightly from 4 to 7 PM drinks are discounted. On Wednesday and Thursday a pianist helps put you in the mood from 6 PM, Friday and Saturday from 8 PM.

Top of the Sixes, Tishman Building, 666 Fifth Avenue between East 52nd and East 53rd Streets. (212)757-6662. The bar is open until 10:30 PM.

P.S. Gentlemen, don't miss the rest room, which also boasts a view!

TOP OF THE TOWER

THE TOP OF THE TOWER is not as well known as some of the more famed sky-high boîtes, but this art deco room on the twenty-sixth floor has a hidden-away clandestine air about it. The glass-enclosed rooftop terrace affords views in all directions and is highly conducive to romance at sunset with piano accompaniment. Yet the views are even more breathtaking when the lights of the city are turned way up, so consider this a top spot for a nightcap when you have been to the theater or to dinner and you want the night to last. Face north and you have the glittering Queensboro and Triboro bridges in your view; gaze south and see the Empire State and Chrysler buildings, also aglow.

Top of the Tower, Beekman Tower Hotel, 3 Mitchell Place, First Avenue at East 49th Street. (212)355-7300. OPEN daily 5 PM to 2 AM.

RAINBOW ROOM

THE RAINBOW ROOM, opened in 1934, was the first large dining and dancing establishment atop a modern commercial skyscraper, and it remains the classiest, most nostalgic of all Manhattan aeries. From the moment you emerge from the elevator on the sixty-fifth floor you are enveloped in quintessential New York elegance. In fact, it is so theatrically elegant you might feel as if you've walked on stage—in a Noel Coward play, of course. You veritably float down the stairs to *the* Room—two stories high with twenty-four floor-to-ceiling windows commanding spectacular views of the Chrysler Building to the southeast, Central Park to the north, and the Statue of Liberty to the south. Three terraces of tables surround the dance floor, which slowly turns beneath a crystal teardrop chandelier and a domed ceiling with hundreds of twinkling rainbow-colored lights, synchronized with the sound system. You will dance—no, glide—to the music of a twelve-piece orchestra, like Joan Crawford and Franchot Tone did no their honeymoon, where Liz Taylor and Richard Burton fox-trotted during their first marriage (to one another). Then you will dine on such classics as oysters Rockefeller, steak tartare, and for dessert baked Alaska for two, flamed at your table; no doubt a glass of champagne will touch your lips as well. Be prepared to spend $200 for the experience, including a $20 per person entertainment charge (yes, it's worth it).

The Rainbow Room, 30 Rockefeller Plaza, 65th floor. (212)632-5000. OPEN Tuesday through Saturday for pretheater dinner 5:30 to 6:30 PM, dinner and dancing 6:30 to 10:30 PM, supper 10:30 PM to midnight, with dancing until 1 AM. Sunday Dinner 6 to 9 PM, with dancing until 11 PM. Jacket and tie required. See also Rainbow Promenade Restaurant/Bar (#122) and Rainbow and Stars (#123).

P.S. You can go early and enjoy the spectacular surroundings and a splendid three-course dinner with complimentary music but without the dancing—a relative bargain at $38.50.

Rainbow Promenade Restaurant/Bar

For a less expensive taste of the elegance the Rainbow Room represents, proceed to the promenade, which runs along the south side of the sixty-fifth floor of 30 Rockefeller Plaza and faces Lower Manhattan. There you can find drinks and economical "Little Meals" like pastrami cured salmon served on pita ($12), a grilled chicken sandwich ($13.50), or a burger and fries ($14); or, for two, a pretheater "Feast for Sharing" ($15) with a sunset chaser. But to make absolutely certain an evening spent elsewhere ends on a high romantic note, add a nightcap at the gorgeous serpentine bar with Normal Bel Geddes' evocative 1939 model of an ocean liner suspended above it and the city night as backdrop. The Empire State Building seems close enough to touch. This has to be the most romantic bar in town (and it gets more so as the night progresses). The cocktail menu is a veritable Baedecker of aphrodisiacs, with such classics as a Between the Sheets, and, of course, a Manhattan, and seasonal creations by mixologist extraordinaire Dale DeGroff, such as a Blood and Sand (scotch, cherry herring, sweet vermouth, and orange). If there aren't too many ahead of you, wait for one of the window tables for two or the cozy terraced booth opposite the bar. I promise you, there isn't an unromantic nook anywhere in this restored rainbow.

Rainbow Promenade Restaurant/Bar. OPEN Monday through Thursday 3 PM to 1 AM, Friday and Saturday 4 PM to 2 AM, Sunday noon to 11 PM, Sunday brunch noon to 2:30 PM. Jacket required.

RAINBOW AND STARS

THIS STUNNING LITTLE SKY-HIGH CABARET, seating 100 for two shows nightly, perfectly captures the promise of the glamour of New York at night. Dinner is required at the early show, so I prefer to go at 10 PM, order a glass of champagne ($9 to $12 a glass) and the caviar sampler ($25) and at 11 PM be bewitched by the likes of Tony Bennett, Rosemary Clooney, Karen Akers, Maureen McGovern, or Mel Tormé performing, with the New York night and the panorama of upper Manhattan as backup. It's such a love-ly—and memorable—way to spend an evening.

Rainbow and Stars, 30 Rockefeller Plaza, 65th floor. (212)632-5000. Shows Tuesday through Saturday 8:30 and 11 PM. A-la-carte dinner from 6:30 PM, supper from 10 PM. Cover charge $35; no minimum charge. Jacket and tie required.

CAFE CARLYLE

NEVER WAS THERE a more fortuitous marriage of person and place than urbane entertainer Bobby Short and the discreetly sophisticated Café Carlyle. Twenty-seven years after the initial pair-ing, the two have come to epitomize New York style and savoir faire. The intimate café with its comfy, salmon-colored upholstered banquettes and the sumptuous wraparound mural by the French painter Marcel Vertes is the inspired setting for the never-short-of-sublime Mr. Short.

Though this jewel of a cabaret seats seventy at each show (and there is never an empty seat), you will swear he's singing just for the two of you. Short, a consummate showman, raconteur, and musicologist, quickly seduces not only with his distinctive raspy yet elegant vocal renditions of classics like "Body and Soul," "Hooray for Love," and "I've Got a Crush on You" but with his intimate knowledge of Cole Porter, George Gershwin, Fats Waller, and Bessie Smith and the times they lived in. For one hour you are privy to and part of a world you have only seen depicted in films, and if you weren't in love when you arrived, you will be when you leave. You can opt to dine at either of the two shows or merely enjoy drinks. Make reservations well in advance unless you want to try your luck at snaring one of the ten seats at the small bar.

Café Carlyle, Carlyle Hotel, 35 East 76th Street at Madison Avenue. (212)744-1600. Bobby Short is in residence every year September through New Year's Eve and April through June. Shows Tuesday through Saturday 8:45 and 10:45 PM. $35 cover charge.

P.S. When Bobby Short is on hiatus from the Café Carlyle there are a few new regulars who make marvelous use of the room. They include three dynamite ladies—the inimitable Barbara Cook, the scintillating Dixie Carter, and the sizzling Eartha Kitt.

THE OAK ROOM AT THE ALGONQUIN

THIS SUPPER CLUB is the "real thing"—a cabaret with a past. In the legendary hotel's dimly candlelit oasis of yesterday it's easy to invoke a rich romantic mood. So settle side by side into the cozy red velvet banquette and listen to the likes of Andrea Marcovicci, a regular who sings of love found and love lost, or the legendary Julie Wilson singing the songs of Gershwin, Porter, Rodgers, and Hart, who are all very much at home in the Oak Room. You'll feel as if time has stopped.

The Oak Room at the Algonquin, 59 West 44th Street. (212)840-6800. One show Tuesday through Thursday at 9 PM, Friday and Saturday also at 11:30 PM. The early show requires that you dine ($18 to $24) dinner served from 7 PM. At the late show there is a $25 minimum charge for drinks. At both shows there is a $30 music charge.

CAFE PIERRE

126

WHEN LIFE WAS SIMPLER and options fewer nearly all of New York's finest hotels offered dinner and dancing, and then came disco. . . . But now it's once again possible to delight in a leisurely dinner or late night supper accompanied by dancing under the painted clouds of this cozy hotel room. Starting at 9 o'clock, Kathleen Landis and a trio provide the musical impetus for you to dance check to cheek. If dining in this romantic albeit pricey atmosphere is beyond your means, dine elsewhere and then pop in at the bar for a classic cocktail and a dance. This also makes a classy post-theater stop when you want an evening to last just a little bit longer.

Café Pierre, Hotel Pierre, Fifth Avenue at 61st Street. (212)940-8185. Trio and dancing every Thursday, Friday, and Saturday from 9 PM to 1 AM. There is a music charge of $10 per person at the bar, none for those who are dining. Jacket and tie required.

THE CHESTNUT ROOM AT TAVERN ON THE GREEN

YET ANOTHER REASON to go to Central Park. One of the best—and without doubt the most dazzling—jazz clubs in town resides within Tavern on the Green. Here, with a view of lantern-garnished garden greenery outside the generous windows, top-flight jazz musicians and you get to benefit from a state of the art sound system, a $95,000 Steinway D grand, and a spectacular romantic setting replete with candlelight. The no minimum policy means you can just have a drink or coffee and be solidly entertained, and the no dress requirement means you can be spontaneous about it. In sum, the Chestnut Room makes for an impressive live entertainment date night on the town without having to cash in your IRA.

The Chestnut Room at Tavern on the Green, Central Park at West 67th Street. (212)873-3200. Two shows nightly Tuesday through Thursday, Sunday at 8 and 9:30 PM, Friday and Saturday 8:30 and 10 PM. Cover charge starts at $18.50 weekdays, $24.50 weekends; no minimum.

LOVE BITES OF
THE APPLE

Restaurant Key

Restaurants are listed in alphabetical order. The key to pricing indicates the cost of an à-la-carte dinner for two without wine, tax, or gratuity (they do not take into consideration prix-fixe specials as well as the lower price of lunch and brunch).

$	$35 or less
$$	$36 to $60
$$$	$60 to $75
$$$$	$76 to $100
$$$$+	More than $100

Unless otherwise noted all major credit cards are honored.

Note: There are more dining choices in the following chapters: Love and Tea in the Afternoon, New York at Night: Isn't It Romantic?, and A Winter's Tale.

*N*ew Yorkers are passionate about dining out. Each of us has a favorite spot we recommend to everyone, and some of us have a secret place we're reluctant to share with anyone—except perhaps someone special. The list of New York's thousands of dining establishments shortens dramatically when it comes to finding one with romance on the menu. And although the definition of what is romantic may be subjective, when it comes to romantic dining there are certain givens. First, a restaurant has to be relatively tranquil. Although not necessarily intimate, it should be a place where the two of you can get lost in one another (that rules out trendy). The food has to be good by New York standards, though if it's casual and reasonably priced it need not merit four stars. Other romantic amenities include either a to-die-for view, a working fireplace in winter, a secluded garden or patio in summer, perhaps a piano bar—a lucky few have all of these. If a restaurant has none of the aforementioned, then it must boast the ability to transport the two of you to somewhere else—preferably Italy or France—or, conversely, it must flaunt an unequivocal Manhattan magic. All of the restaurants recommended in this chapter fit one or more of the above criteria. The price range is wide, ranging from reasonable to sky high, but each of them happily serves a generous helping of romance—at no extra charge.

AMERICAN FESTIVAL CAFE

(128) THE MORE CASUAL OF THE TWO major dining establishments on the perimeter of the skating rink in Rockefeller Plaza, the American Festival Café is a spot many New Yorkers tend to disdain as just for tourists. They're missing out on a charming and romantic spot for a leisurely lunch or dinner or for a cozy hot chocolate (off-peak hours) in winter while watching the skaters from a rink-side window table, or, best of all, for an early (starting at 7:30 AM weekdays) alfresco breakfast in summer when the rink becomes a gardenlike, umbrella-shaded oasis at the foot of midtown's canyons. In warm weather there is no prettier breakfast venue in the city. There's also a long outdoor bar, which you should keep in mind for an alfresco tropical drink after work or for a late-night (until midnight) snack when the evening is lovely and the waters of the Prometheus fountain provide a cooling backdrop.

American Festival Café, 20 West 50th Street between Fifth and Sixth Avenues, lower concourse. (212)246-6699. Breakfast Monday through Friday 7:30 to 10:30 AM, Saturday and Sunday 9 to 10:30 AM. Lunch Monday through Friday 11 AM to 4 PM, Saturday and Sunday 11 AM to 3:30 PM. Dinner Monday through Sunday 4 to 11 PM. $$

P.S. An alternative to breakfast at the American Festival Café is Savories, just around the bend, where you can dine on essentially the same breakfast fare in more casual surroundings at lower prices. It offers the same view, and in summer, outside tables as well.

Savories, 30 Rockefeller Center, lower concourse. (212)246-6457. Breakfast Monday through Friday 7 to 11 AM. $

AU TROQUET

A ROMANTIC OASIS on a corner in the far West Village—that's as Parisian as a New York bistro can get. Au Troquet is small, only sixteen tables, and with its lace curtains, antiques, flowers, and watercolors it conveys a palpable warmth and intimate charm. The changing menu is limited but enticing and of a hearty nature, so keep Au Troquet in mind on a cold winter night when you want to be warmed inside and out. Among the choices are cassoulet, bouillabaisse, fresh salmon marinated with basil, rack of lamb, escargots with garlic butter. For dessert there is always a freshly baked tart.

Au Troquet, 328 West 12th Street at Greenwich Street. (212)924-3413. Dinner daily 6 to 11 PM. $$

BARBETTA

THIS LONG-RUNNING THEATER ROW restaurant, located in a stunning town house, is outfitted with antiques and sumptuous fabrics, with cozy love seats in the lounge, its grand main dining room dominated by an eighteenth-century Piedmontese crystal chandelier. The Piedmont specialties, the most pleasing of the dishes offered, include a cold minestrone, risotto with mushrooms and bits of liver, tagliarini di campagna, and grilled baby chicken; for dessert there's a wonderful zabaglione with fruit.

Barbetta is an extremely elegant if sometimes rushed pretheater choice. The $39 prix-fixe five-course dinner, served from 5 to 7 PM, and the restaurant's proximity to the theaters draw quite a crowd, which limits its romantic possibilities. Ah, but after 8 o'clock, when the curtain goes up on

Broadway, you are rewarded for not having tickets because this is a positively gracious, albeit more expensive dinner venue at this hour, especially in spring and summer, when you may dine in the exquisite rear garden. With its stone floor, stately trees, magnolia, jasmin, and gardenia blossoms, and a cherub-decorated fountain, it's impossibly romantic, not only in the evening but also at lunchtime. At either meal you will be inclined to linger in the garden, incredulous that you are in midtown Manhattan when it feels so much like Rome.

Barbetta, 321 West 46th Street between Eighth and Ninth Avenues. (212)246-9171. Lunch Monday through Saturday noon to 2 PM, dinner 5 to 11:30 PM. $$$$

P.S. If you choose, you may return after the theater to have your coffee and dessert.

BAROLO

THIS CAVERNOUS, cosmopolitan, and often cacophonous northern Italian restaurant in SoHo would be an unlikely choice for a romantic dinner for two were it not for its glorious, spacious walled-in garden. With its nine spot-lighted cherry trees (spectacular in April when they are in bloom) and terra-cotta floors, this may be the city's most dramatic dining garden.

Upon arrival you'll walk through two large dining areas to reach the garden; if it's early enough, you may get to choose between sitting in the garden or on the balcony that overlooks the garden. If you arrive at the height of the dinner rush, or without a reservation, you may have to wait at the bar located in the garden—not a bad setting in which to wait.

Fittingly, the pastas are Barolo's strong suit, as are its

roasted and sautéed dishes. Among the extremely satisfying choices are gnocchi with pesto sauce, green beans, and potatoes, and rigatoni with eggplant and ricotta. The two of you can split either one as a first course and then follow with grilled salmon with mustard sauce or grilled veal chop with Shitake mushrooms. I have no doubt you will also devour the basket of excellent focaccia that is set before you. Linger over your wine, perhaps one of their fine Barolos, but meander to somewhere else in SoHo for dessert.

As for where you choose to sit, though sitting in the garden itself is tempting, the balcony with its smaller tables built for two is more intimate and comes with an option the garden does not afford—shelter from the rain. Dining on the protected balcony while gazing at the deserted garden as rain dances on the tables and the terra-cotta floor is pure magic, something Hollywood might have dreamed up but is reality in romantic New York.

Barolo, 398 West Broadway between Spring and Broome Streets. (212)226-1102. OPEN Sunday through Thursday noon to midnight, Friday and Saturday until 1 AM. $$$

THE BLACK SHEEP

LONG TUCKED AWAY in the far West Village, the Black Sheep has remained steadfastly unchanged through the years, and that's good news because this purveyor of rustic French country fare has always been inviting with its lace curtains, brick walls, and faux fireplace in winter. The two dining areas are dimly lighted for romance, with candles on every table. The five-course prix-fixe dinner (averaging $28) is an astonishingly good value. You begin with a generous portion of crudités, followed by soup, country pâté, or an appetizer special. Among the main courses representing seasonal offerings are pastas, roast chicken stuffed with couscous, braised pork with red cabbage, and provençal fish stew. For dessert there is a solid chocolate truffle cake to satisfy any sweet tooth. The list of American and French wines is extensive and well chosen. In sum, the Black Sheep is the kind of restaurant you would conjure up on a cold evening in winter when you want to be casual and cozy, but eat and drink well. It's also a good choice for Sunday brunch.

The Black Sheep, 342 West 11th Street at Washington Street. (212)242-1010. Dinner Monday through Thursday 6 to 11 PM, Friday and Saturday until midnight, Sunday until 10:30. Weekend brunch noon to 3:30 PM. American Express only. $$

THE BOATHOUSE CAFE

THE RESTORED LOEB BOATHOUSE on Central Park Lake is as bucolic a place as you can find without leaving the city. This sylvan setting offers soothing views of lush greenery and placid water, without a car in sight or the hum of an air conditioner in the background. The Boathouse Café is the most romantically beautiful place to dine outdoors in summer, best just as the sun is beginning to set. It's especially calm on weekday evenings, and because the dining area is under a tall canopy equipped with ceiling fans, this venue should not be ruled out even if the weather is less than perfect. A rainy lunch date on the lake is a scenic designer's dream, and one you both will long remember. In the evening there's even an authentic Venetian gondola, *The Daughter of Venice,* for rent, and I suggest taking a twenty-minute glide on the lake between your main course and dessert—it's pure magic (#70).

141

The Boathouse Café serves unlimited amounts of the best focaccia in town, and with a dish of olive oil for dipping, eating it becomes a sensual experience. The contemporary American menu has a seafood emphasis, featuring crispy crab roll, grilled seafood risotto and seared salmon with wilted spinach. No matter what comes before, save room—the desserts are glorious. Service is earnest, if slow, but I promise you will not mind lingering.

Boathouse Café, Loeb Boathouse, Central Park Lake at 74th Street (enter the park at East 72nd Street). (212)517-3623. OPEN April through October, Monday through Thursday 11:30 AM to 10 PM, Friday 11:30 AM to 11 PM, Saturday 11 AM to 11 PM, Sunday 11 AM to 9 PM. $$$

P.S. Beginning at 7 PM, a charming motorized trolley, departing from Fifth Avenue and West 72nd Street, will shuttle you into and out of the park, so the wisdom of walking through the park at night is not a consideration.

THE BOX TREE RESTAURANT AND INN

THE BOX TREE offers an intimate townhouse setting for fine French food in a rarified, if somewhat theatrical, atmosphere. There are two ornate dining rooms with hearths and oversized tables and chairs. Dinner here has a formal air, although if you don't mind the stratospheric prices, it is romantic on a grand scale.

There is the proverbial candlelight, a fire in the hearth, and a single red rose at each place setting; the menu proffered female guests is without prices, as if the concept of the working woman were foreign to this domain. But there's more than dinner on the $86 prix-fixe menu. The Box Tree is also an upscale inn, and many of the diners are also guests, staying in the enormously expensive and opulently furnished thirteen rooms, each boasting fur throws and working fireplaces. When the occasion is extremely important and money is no object, the most romantic way to enjoy the Box Tree is to book one of the palatial (in style, not size) rooms as well as a place at the table: Memories are made of this.

The Box Tree Restaurant and Inn, 242 East 49th Street between Second and Third Avenues. (212)758-8320. Lunch Sunday through Friday noon to 2 PM, dinner nightly 6 to 11 PM. $$$$+ Rooms: Sunday through Thursday $170–210, Friday and Saturday $270–310; $100 of which is credited to dinner.

P.S. Lunch at The Box Tree (3 courses, $42) is an intimate quiet affair.

CAFE DES ARTISTES

THE CAFE DES ARTISTES is usually at the top of every New Yorker's list of romantic dining rooms. Incredibly, it's one of those places where you can never go wrong; it can be intimate at lunch, at dinner, at brunch, for any occasion, for any reason, in any season. It never fails to enchant all who enter, whether for the first or fiftieth time.

A large part of the allure of the Café des Artistes is the feast it offers the eyes as well as the palate. There are the glorious floral arrangements, the close-up view of the sumptuous desserts upon entering, the burnished wood paneling, and the murals of those sweetly naughty, ever-young and nubile, naked nymphs, frolicking just as they did when they were painted in 1934 and 1942 by Howard Chandler Christy. The illustrator and portrait painter was in 1917 one of the earliest residents of the then newly constructed Hotel des Artistes, a residential building boasting a ballroom, swimming pool, squash court, and the grand ground-floor restaurant, where tenants sent down fresh ingredients to the kitchen to be cooked and then returned via the dumb waiter. The restaurant, as current owner George Lang describes it in the brochure about the café, was fashioned after the English Ordinary, a bistro with a limited menu utilizing foods available at the market. This is the tradition Mr. Lang employs to seduce diners like Paul Newman, Kathleen Turner, Peter Jennings, and Isaac Stern into returning again and again. Among the signature dishes are pot-au-feu, cassoulet, rack of lamb with a basil crust, a plate of four salmons, and steak au poivre. There is a three-course prix-fixe lunch for $19.50 and dinner for $32. As befitting what could be mistaken for an Old World European café, the desserts are among the city's best, and the sampler plate for the two of you to share is the perfect finale to the meal.

A word about where to sit to best savor the surroundings and each other: The back room with its cozy booths around the mahogany bar is the most intimate area, but don't rule out the dark middle room, where an eyeful of those nymphs may inspire you to frolic as well. Or you could choose the nearly secluded niche in the otherwise noisier front room where Anjelica Houston and Woody Allen played cards and lunched in *Manhattan Murder Mystery*.

Café des Artistes, 1 West 67th Street between Central Park West and Columbus Avenue. (212)877-3500. Lunch Monday through Friday noon to 3 PM. Dinner Monday through Saturday 5:30 PM to 12:30 AM, Sunday 5:30 to 11 PM. Brunch Saturday noon to 3 PM, Sunday 10 AM to 4 PM. Jackets required after 5 PM. $$$

P.S. Mr. Lang, this is my love note to you: No one practices the art of café better than Café des Artistes.

Cafe Nicholson

AS FANCIFUL AS A RESTAURANT can be, as quixotic as an owner can be—Café Nicholson is in a category of New York restaurants all its own. Tucked beneath the ramp to the 59th Street Bridge, this exceptionally personal place belongs to one John Nicholson, who produces delightfully simple fare: herbed roast chicken, filet mignon, crab cakes, cheese soufflé, filet of sole, and a delectable if (for me) too-small chocolate soufflé for dessert. The three-course prix-fixe dinner ($36), which includes wine, is served in a glorious dining room, the walls of which are covered in ornate nineteenth-century handpainted tiles. The space is filled with antique furnishings, pottery, and paintings, all of which contribute to the feeling that you're a very special dinner guest in the mansion of a wealthy aristocrat. The only drawback to this most fanciful of dining experiences is the inevitable wanderlust of Mr. Nicholson, who takes off for the summer and various other times during the year. Since he is the chef, host, and server, when John's gone Café Nicholson is shuttered. So when you feel you want a rather uncommon romantic evening out, call and you will either get reservations for dinner or a recording essentially saying "gone fishing."

Café Nicholson, 323 East 58th Street between First and Second Avenues. (212)355-6769. OPEN (as far as it can be pinned down) Wednesday through Saturday, 6:30 to 9 PM. Never open in summer. $$$$

Capsouto Freres

This spacious and handsome restaurant is ensconced in an 1891 landmark building on a remote corner in TriBeCa. In the evening, when you finally spy the place amid all the desolation, it's as if a stage set has been revealed by a rising curtain. The welcome is warm and the crowd convivial. The former warehouse with high ceilings, brick walls, wood floors, and cast-iron columns is softened by mirrors, lace curtains, flowers, and classical music; in summer there are umbrella-shaded tables on a terrace (a former loading platform). Sunset is an especially romantic time, seen through the west-facing floor to ceiling windows. The choices of country French dishes reflect a nice variety of seasonally fresh ingredients. For example, there is a country-style sausage with warm potatoes; a terrine of eggplant, roasted peppers, and goat cheese; and a poached salmon with warm fresh-herb vinaigrette. For dessert you must have one of the delectable soufflés.

Though Capsouto Frères is not easy to find, its remoteness is part of what makes it so romantic; perhaps in deference to your tenacity in seeking out their establishment, the Capsouto brothers encourage lingering.

Capsouto Frères, 451 Washington Street at Watts Street. (212)966-4900. Lunch Tuesday through Sunday noon to 3 PM. Dinner Sunday through Thursday 6 to 11:30 PM, Friday and Saturday until 12:30 AM. The bar is open until 4 AM. Weekend brunch noon to 3 PM. $$$

P.S. Weekend brunch at Capsouto Frères is a great first date coupled with a stroll around TriBeCa.

CHANTAL CAFE

A NARROW DINING SPACE in a turn-of-the century brownstone makes for an informal and welcoming pretheater dining spot. Chantal Café is a most authentic French bistro in an area of Manhattan that used to be a small French quarter, and it's reasonably priced. Head for the appealing back room with its skylight, beamed ceiling, and brick walls. The bistro menu offerings include mussels provençal, couscous, cassoulet, roast leg of lamb with rosemary, poached salmon, veal shank niçoise, steak pommes frites, and, for dessert, a splendid floating island. Friday is the day to have a hearty bouillabaisse with lobster. Every week night there is a wonderfully good-value three-course pretheater dinner ($20) served from 5:30 to 7 PM, as well as a reasonably priced wine list. Of course, the most romantic time to dine here is between 8 and 10 PM—when everyone else is at the theater. In sum, Chantal Café offers good food and charm without flattening your wallet.

Chantal Café, 257 West 55th Street between Broadway and Eighth Avenue. (212)246-7076. Lunch Monday through Friday 11:30 AM to 3 PM. Dinner Monday through Thursday 5:30 to 10:30 PM, Friday and Saturday until 11:30 PM. $$

CHEZ JOSEPHINE

THIS LIVELY SPOT is an ode to the famed American cabaret star Josephine Baker, who made an indelible impression on Paris in the twenties, by one of her many adopted children, Jean-Claude. The mood of that time and place are perfectly captured by the vivid and exotic decor, and the

147

result is an atmosphere that is veritably intoxicating. Let the pretheater crowd vacate the premises before you settle into a languid dinner of reliably zesty French bistro food. Choices include a delectable boudin noir with red cabbage, lobster cassoulet, goat-cheese ravioli, or steak au poivre. Linger over coffee and crème brulée or an after-dinner drink amid the period palm tree lamps while the piano player serenades with old jazz and blues tunes. If you're willing, you will surely be transported to Paris, circa 1925.

Chez Josephine, 414 West 42nd Street between Ninth and Tenth Avenues. (212)594-1925. Dinner Monday through Saturday 6 PM to midnight. The bar is open until 2 AM. $$$

P.S. Chez Josephine is a perfect pick for a *très intime* posttheater supper. Table no. 18 next to the piano is Jean-Claude's personal pick for most romantic spot.

THE CORNELIA STREET CAFE

CASUAL AND COZY on a nearly hidden Greenwich Village side street, the Cornelia Street Café features outdoor tables in warm weather and a fireplace in winter. What an ideal place to while away an early summer morning over great cappuccino and a flaky croissant, or on a lazy spring or autumn afternoon to enjoy a fine pasta salad with Zito's irresistible whole-wheat bread, or in winter to savor a fireside dinner of surprisingly good specials. There's even poetry spoken here. How much more romantic can an informal, inexpensive café get?

Cornelia Street Café, 29 Cornelia Street between Bleecker and West 4th Streets. (212)989-9319. OPEN daily 9 AM to 1 AM, weekend brunch 9:30 AM to 4:30 PM. $

THE CLOISTER CAFE

THE CAPTIVATING COURTYARD of this café is the main draw. I've never heard people talk about the food, no doubt because they have been so thoroughly beguiled by this oasis in the midst of the otherwise unromantic East Village. In the evening the garden, under a canopy of twinkling white lights and tall leafy trees, soothes with the sound of a gurgling ground-level fountain and the sight of ivy-covered brick walls and flowering plants everywhere. During the day, though less magical, it is a cool spot to get away to for a big bowl of café au lait and a pastry. When the garden is not open (November to April) the interior of the café itself has a dark moodiness engendered by stained glass, flickering candles, and the warmth of a pot-bellied stove.

Cloister Café, 238 East 9th Street between Second and Third Avenues. (212)777-9128. OPEN Sunday through Thursday 11 AM to 1 AM, Friday and Saturday until 2 AM. Weekend brunch 11 AM to 5 PM. No credit cards. $

HUDSON RIVER CLUB

HUDSON RIVER CLUB is one of the most alluring places to drink and dine in the Wall Street area. The three-tiered dining room, in muted tones with tapestry banquettes and polished brash accents, provides a wondrous view of the charming North Cove Harbor Marina just below—and the vista extends beyond, to the Hudson, the upper harbor, and the Statue of Liberty and Ellis Island in the distance. Timed for sunset, your predinner cocktails at a window table against this backdrop are even more intoxicating. The restaurant, which celebrates the bounty of the New York State Hudson Valley, is deservedly popular with the World Financial and Trade Center lunch crowd, but after office hours the entire area in general, and this restaurant in particular, take on a decidedly tranquil air. For all of the formality of the surroundings, dinner here, especially during the week, is a relaxed, intimate affair by candlelight. The food is beautifully prepared and presented, with much fish and seasonal game featured. Standouts are salmon in woven potatoes, smoked quail and goat-cheese salad and maple-coated roast duckling accompanied by a wild rice custard. The desserts—especially the "Chocolate Tower"—deserve special mention. Worth noting, too, is the superb service, which is accommodating and attentive but not intrusive, so that you are left to savor the food, the surroundings, and each other. The staff here is to be commended.

Hudson River Club, 250 Vesey Street in the World Financial Center, second level. (212)786-1500. Lunch Monday through Saturday 11:30AM to 2:30 PM, dinner Monday through Saturday 5:30 to 9:30 PM. Jacket required. $$$$+

P.S. To prolong the pleasure of dining at the Hudson River Club, after dinner take a promenade along the Hudson River Esplanade (#45)—where, but for the landmarks, you might be anywhere in the world.

JEZEBEL

NOTHING ON THE OUTSIDE prepares you for the delight you experience upon entering the mood piece of a restaurant called Jezebel. The fringed lamp shades and silk shawls (remnants of the owner's former life as a purveyor of vintage clothing), languid ceiling fans, lawn swings, wicker tables and chairs, and Oriental wall hangings all summon up a vision of a New Orleans bordello. Talk about being transported! It's a perfect setting for food to satisfy the soul, including yummy cornbread, spare ribs, honey chicken, shrimp Creole, and deep-fried whole fish—all accompanied by grits, yams, and sweet potato pie; and for dessert there's bread pudding. To really enjoy the setting, go after the curtain rises at nearby theaters. The soulful jazz piano music starts at about 9 PM, and you'll really get in the mood. Even if you've dined elsewhere before going to the theater, Jezebel is a great place to have a sexy post-theater drink instead of fighting the crowds for a cab.

Jezebel, 630 Ninth Avenue at West 45th Street. (212)582-1045. OPEN daily 5:30 to 11:45 PM. The bar is open until 1 AM. American Express only. $$

LA COLOMBE D'OR

THIS SMALL, ROMANTIC RESTAURANT has long been a fine dining destination, and under the new ownership of celebrated chef Wayne Nish it has become even more popular. The intimate brownstone setting, with two dining areas, is provençal rustic with terra-cotta floors, brick walls, tin ceilings, and comfortable banquettes covered in a pretty print fabric. Its location out of midtown ensures that lunching here at noon can be a quiet affair, as is early evening dining. For the purpose of romance, request table 32, 14, or 12.

The reassuringly robust regional fare includes flavorful bouillabaisse, grilled calves' liver, socca roulade, and confit of duck, and the $24.95 three-course prix fixe at lunch is a good value. Service at all times is charmingly attentive, but La Colombe D'Or respects your privacy, especially if you look as though you're in love. It's ideal for a lunchtime assignation.

La Colombe D'Or, 134 East 26th Street between Lexington and Third Avenues. (212)689-0666. Lunch Monday through Friday noon to 2:30 PM. Dinner Monday through Thursday 6 to 10:30 PM, Friday and Saturday until 11 PM, Sunday 5:30 to 9:30 PM. $$$

LA GRENOUILLE

145) LA GRENOUILLE is still the most romantic of New York's long-time classic French restaurants. The dining room with its red velvet banquettes and those little lamps with silk shades is enchanting. The spectacular floral arrangements are breathtaking as always, and the classic French cuisine is better than ever. The inevitable celebrities are seated up front at lunch, but for a more intimate dining experience go to La Grenouille for dinner. Savor the ravioli filled with lobster; saddle of lamb stuffed with zucchini, carrots, and leeks; the airy pike dumplings; or sole mousse. And for dessert share the marvelous order-ahead Grand Marnier soufflé. Unless you've won the lottery you won't be dining here nightly, but La Grenouille should be near the top of your list when you have something very special to celebrate and want to dine exceptionally well.

La Grenouille, 3 East 52nd Street between Fifth and Madison Avenues. (212)752-1495. Lunch Tuesday through Saturday noon to 2:30 PM, dinner 6 to 11:30 PM. $$$$+

P.S. The private dining atelier of La Grenouille may be one of the most romantic reasons to become a millionaire.

LA MANGEOIRE

146

THE PRETTY, RUSTIC FRENCH COUNTRY SETTING of La Mangeoire provides an instant mood change from the bustle of midtown. The restaurant has been a long-time favorite of many who live and work in the area, but rather unsung as a dining destination, and that's a shame. It's one of the few midtown restaurants where you can actually have a romantic weekday lunch. The French provençal decor with thatched ceiling, dried floral arrangements, tile and stucco walls, and dark beams is charming. The secluded dining area to the left of the tiny bar with seating on three sides is the most romantic place to perch, especially before 7 PM or after 9 PM. Specialties include bouillabaisse, ravioli niçoise and charlotte of lamb and eggplant. Whether at lunch or dinner, you will be well attended and well fed, all at a leisurely pace. And as a bonus the reasonable two-course prix-fixe lunch or dinner ($17.50 and $19.50, respectively) belies the high-rent neighborhood.

La Mangeoire, 1008 Second Avenue between East 53rd and East 54th Streets. (212)759-7086. Lunch Monday through Friday noon to 2:30 PM. Dinner Monday through Saturday 6 to 11 PM, Sunday 5:30 to 10 PM. $$

LA METAIRIE

LA METAIRIE has always been a most appealing French country restaurant, but there was a time before expansion when only ten tables constituted the entire restaurant, and I confess you really had to be very much in love not to become increasingly claustrophobic as dinner progressed. Even now some feel it's a bit too cozy.

The restaurant exudes a whitewashed French farmhouse charm, with dark wooden beams, dried floral arrangements, farmyard artifacts, provençal paisley-print seat coverings, flickering candlelight, and a pair of cooing doves. How can anyone with a heart resist? Though there is no outdoor dining area the French windows are flung open on warm days and balmy evenings, and the effect enhances the romantic aura. Start with a kir royale, and then leisurely move on to some delightful rustic French fare. Try the garlic flan for an appetizer (make sure you both have it), then choose from grilled tuna steak, sliced breast of duck, grilled cornish hen, or rack of lamb. Linger over your crème brulée and coffee. A big plus for Le Métairie is that it serves until midnight and later on the weekend.

La Métairie, 189 West 10th Street at West 4th Street (just west of Seventh Avenue). (212)989-0343. Dinner Sunday through Thursday 5 PM to midnight, Friday and Saturday until 1 AM. American Express only. $$$

LATTANZI

LOCATED IN A brownstone on Restaurant Row, Lattanzi represents an appealing lower-priced pretheater choice, especially in summer when you can sit at one of the four umbrella-shaded tables in the garden. In winter the restaurant is a cozy brick-walled grotto, but always request the more intimate rear patio room with skylights.

The best time to dine here for a serene twosome is at lunch (not matinee days) or dinner after 8 o'clock, when the theater crowd has left. The menu presents many traditional dishes of the old Roman Jewish quarter, and the fare is light and simple, yet interesting. The emphasis is on pastas with fresh vegetables and on meats, fish, and chicken that have been marinated and then sautéed and stewed. All are accented with fresh rosemary, bay leaves, garlic, olive oil, and white vinegar. Specialties include artichokes Jewish style, deep fried in boiling olive oil infused with garlic cloves; poached red snapper topped with raisins and pine nuts; dried beef with zucchini marinated in olive oil; and chicken roasted in rosemary and garlic. Desserts include a creamy Napoleon, among other tasty treats all made on the premises.

Lattanzi, 361 West 46th Street between Eighth and Ninth Avenues. (212)315-0980. Lunch Monday through Friday noon to 11 PM. Dinner Monday through Thursday 5 to 11 PM, Friday and Saturday until midnight. $$

155

LE CHANTILLY

149 A SUMPTUOUS AND CIVILIZED PLACE to dine, Le Chantilly features murals of its namesake chateau in the Loire Valley of France, comfortable banquettes, and tables well spaced for privacy. Dinner is the time to come for quiet romance (especially if you request a corner banquette in the front dining area) and excellent food. The kitchen has recently come under the aegis of David Ruggerio, who has made Le Chantilly even better than the gracious place it has been for more than thirty years.

The seasonal menu now reflects the flavorings of the Mediterranean, with emphasis on dishes like crab ravioli, quail risotto, braised salmon over herbed couscous, Maine lobster with crisp noodle cake, and spicy carrots. Also offered at dinner is a five-course vegetable tasting, which changes daily depending upon availability. Desserts are nothing short of amazing: One of you must order the chocolate piano filled with hazelnuts, almonds, and cocoa sorbet and the other the white chocolate Humphrey Bogart hat!

Le Chantilly, 106 East 57th Street between Park and Lexington Avenues. (212)751-2931. Lunch Monday through Saturday noon to 3 PM. Dinner Monday through Saturday 5:30 to 11:30 PM, Sunday 4:30 to 10 PM. Jacket required. $$$$

LE REFUGE

150 LOCATED IN AN 1868 TOWN HOUSE on the Upper East Side, the three dining rooms with French provençal antiques, charming paintings, and a profusion of flowers betray a rustic charm, and as the name implies offer a refuge from the city's hurly-burly. Le Refuge is wonderfully located for a "romantic combo" on Friday or Saturday evening with the Metropolitan Museum. The candlelit wooden-beamed back room with brick walls adorned with tapestries provides the most intimate dining and is the best place to have a late supper (10 to 11:30 PM). The country French fare offered on both the printed menu and the specials always pleases; favorites include lobster ravioli, vegetable terrine, shrimps with couscous, and for dessert a wonderful flourless chocolate cake. In summer there's a rear-garden terrace with five umbrella-shaded tables for romantic open-air dining, especially after 9 PM.

Le Refuge, 186 East 82nd Street between Lexington and Third Avenues. (212)861-4505. Lunch daily noon to 2:30 PM, dinner 5 to 11:30 PM. American Express only. $$$

P.S. La Refuge also owns a romantic Bed & Breakfast on City Island (#86).

ONE IF BY LAND, TWO IF BY SEA

151

THIS RESTORED EIGHTEENTH-CENTURY CAR-RIAGE HOUSE, once the residence of Aaron Burr, has always drawn the romantically inclined. The food was once an afterthought, but no longer. The former *sous-chef* of American Place is now serving some of the best seasonally fresh American fare, and he has retained the restaurant's two signature dishes, beef Wellington and rack of lamb. Now you can have your romance and eat well too.

Year-round there are fresh flowers and candlelight, and in winter the two fireplaces add to the romantic glow. Alas, all of this does not come cheap, so you might opt to join the handsome crowd that comes for drinks and show tunes at the piano bar starting at 4 PM and going on until 3 AM. One If By Land . . . is the perfect Greenwich Village nightcap spot.

One If By Land . . . , 17 Barrow Street between Seventh Avenue South and West 4th Street. (212)255-8649. OPEN Sunday through Thursday 5:30 PM to midnight, Friday and Saturday until 1 AM. The bar is open until 3 AM. $$$$

PARIOLI, ROMANISSIMO

152

DINING AT THIS LONG-TIME ITALIAN RESTAU-RANT located in a charming townhouse is a lux-urious experience. The parlor floor boasts two dining rooms, the more formal main one with a fireplace and the smaller glass-enclosed court-yard with a charming fountain; the former is more romantic in winter. The northern Italian menu features seasonal spe-cials, and the well-prepared pastas and risottos are stand-outs, as are the fish entrées. For after dinner, in true Italian style, there is an extensive selection of cheeses, over forty in all. This is an expensive and not easily booked venue, but it's worth a visit, if only once for a very special occasion when you want your romance Italian-style.

Parioli, Romanissimo, 24 East 81st Street between Madison and Fifth Avenues. (212)288-2391. Dinner Tuesday through Saturday 6 to 11 PM Jacket and tie required. $$$$+

PROVENCE

TUCKED AWAY on the cusp between Greenwich Village and SoHo is this rustic bistro with pale-yellow walls, blue-bordered French windows, and dried flowers. Charmingly evocative of its namesake, the environment is as sunny as the region it represents, with commendable cooking season after season. Both the atmosphere and the food are spirited, and the air is redolent with garlic. The bourride, a garlicky Mediterranean fish soup, onion tart, bouillabaisse, roasted chicken in garlic, and glorious crème brulée, draw hordes, so you'll have to choose your moment of romance carefully. Lunch is usually less hectic, and in the summer the enchanting tented garden, with its gurgling stone fountain encircled by flowers, is the place to dine—either for a late lunch (2:30 PM) or a late dinner (10 PM).

Provence delights, not least of all with its moderate prices, and even though it's hard to find a quiet, intimate moment in a place this popular, I'll bet the two of you will leave here smiling.

Provence, 38 MacDougal Street at Prince Street. (212)475-7500. Lunch daily noon to 3 PM, dinner 6 to 11:30 PM. American Express only. $$$

RESTAURANT RAPHAEL

RAPHAEL IS LIKE A JEWEL hidden in plain sight. Not only is it beautiful, in the style of a French country chateau, with a striking vineyard mural, it is also most inviting. And in summer there's a romantic little trellised garden in which to dine. Although it is just steps from the bustle of Fifth Avenue, once you enter Raphael all is serene; there is no clatter, just a quiet, intimate charm. Add to all of this the fact that the former chef of Le Cygne, Jean-Michel Bergougnoux, is now wearing the toque in this kitchen and Raphael should become a must for a romantic lunch or dinner. The seared tuna steak sandwiched between crisp potatoes is a treat, as is the pancake layered with potato purée and thin slices of salmon and caviar studded with whipped cream, onions, and chives, and the succulent roasted duck with passion fruit and polenta with raisins. For dessert the crusty chocolate cake (which uses four different types of chocolate) with its warm center is positively sinful. Be forewarned, à-la-carte lunch or dinner at Raphael is expensive, but you can choose the reasonable pretheater three-course prix fixe ($29).

Restaurant Raphael, 33 West 54th Street between Fifth and Sixth Avenues. (212)582-8993. Lunch Monday through Friday noon to 2:30 PM. Dinner Monday to Saturday 6 to 10:30 PM. Jacket required. $$$$

THE RIVER CAFE

155) THE RIVER CAFE, located on a permanently moored barge in the shadow of the Brooklyn Bridge, is the premier dining destination in Brooklyn. Not only does it serve some of the best American cuisine in the city, but with its glass-enclosed dining room it provides a front row seat for *the* picture-perfect view of Lower Manhattan, especially thrilling at dinner at one of the nine window tables. This is one of the few instances where the food measures up to the view, although there seems to have been a revolving door in the kitchen, where changing chefs is as much a part of the scene as the vista. This is a special-occasion place, and more than a few of those occasions involve popping the question

followed by popping the cork. Keep that in mind fellas—or gals. The six-course tasting menu ($85) is always a good way to limit decisions and plumb what the chef is up to creatively, and for the full effect of the locale, order the Brooklyn Bridge (in chocolate) for dessert. Being in the fortunate position of facing west, the River Café is popular for sunset cocktails either in the indoor patio or in summer outside at an umbrella-shaded table on the spacious waterfront café. The piano bar is also a flawless spot for a romantic rendezvous any night between 6:30 PM and 1 AM.

The River Café, 1 Water Street, Brooklyn. (718)522-5200. Lunch Monday through Friday noon to 2:30 PM. Dinner daily 6 to 11:30 PM. Weekend brunch Saturday noon to 2:30 PM, Sunday 11:30 AM to 2:30 PM. Jacket required. $$$$+

ROETTELE, A.G.

156) THOUGH ENSCONCED in the East Village, Roettele is as far removed from that neighborhood's quirky irreverent style as, say, the Balkans are from Switzerland. A store-front warren of rooms with brick walls and faux grapevine motif conveys a cozy message: It's a comforting place with food to match, and it's decidedly untrendy. The modestly priced menu presents dishes representative of French, Swiss, German, and Italian cuisine; they are by no means light, but they are spirited. There is a house gravlax with a dill-honey-mustard sauce, grilled steak with a peppercorn sauce and potato gratin, sauerbraten with red cabbage and rösti, and salmon baked in a horseradish crust and served with cucumber and crème fraiche. Desserts, which are made on the premises, are enticing, especially the chocolate brownie, which comes sliced in several small pieces—perhaps to assuage guilt.

161

In winter the most romantic place to sit is either in the long dining area in the rear, which has several tables for two along each wall, or in the room with the tiny bar, which has only three tables. If it's a weekday or late in the evening, you may have this dining room, with its exuberant Venetian-glass chandelier, all to yourselves. If dining at Roettele in summer, the *only* place to sit, in love or not, is in the forty-seat garden in the back. Under a trellised grape arbor with votive candles on the paper-covered tables you will feel transported. (For me it was reminiscent of a restaurant in Venice, also with grape arbor, called Loconda Montin) The setting is conducive to romance. Swiss or Italian wine may help to put you in the mood—the rest is up to you.

Roetelle, A.G., 126 East 7th Street between First Avenue and Avenue A. (212)674-4140. Lunch Monday through Saturday noon to 3 PM, dinner 5:30 to 11 PM. $

THE RUSSIAN TEA ROOM

THE RUSSIAN TEA ROOM was founded by a member of the Russian Imperial Ballet as a tea-room in 1926. It served ice cream, pastries, and tea until the end of Prohibition when the vodka began to flow, and flow it still does. The celebrity-filled, festive, year-round red, green, and gold Christmas-decorated landmark is woven into the romantic lore of New York, where restaurants get rated for people-watching as well as for the food. The Russian Tea Room has its detractors, but if you go late and order light you can make this a romantic stop before heading home after Carnegie Hall, the theater, or Lincoln Center. It is best late at night, when an à-la-carte supper menu is served beginning at 9:30 PM. This is the perfect time for vodka (there are now thirty-two varieties), caviar, and the rightly famed buckwheat blini slathered in red-salmon caviar with sour cream. Be sure to request a seat in the main dining room. And what New Yorker is so jaded that he or she won't take a look at the front booth to see if Liza or Misha or Dustin is there?

The Russian Tea Room, 150 West 57th Street between Sixth and Seventh Avenues. (212)265-0947. OPEN Monday through Friday 11:30 AM to 11:30 PM, Saturday and Sunday from 11 AM. $$$

THE SEAGRILL

158) LIKE THE AMERICAN FESTIVAL CAFE, also located in Rockefeller Center, the SeaGrill benefits from a splendid up-close view of skaters on the rink in winter and umbrella-shaded seating in the glorious summer garden from spring through fall.

More expensive and elegant than the American Festival, if the two of you are fish lovers, the SeaGrill is the place for you. Feast on soft-shelled crabs with white asparagus, Maryland crabcakes with lobster and chive sauce, grilled yellowfin tuna seared on hardwood coals, and roast salmon with Dijon sauce. For dessert choose the red-gold-dusted Prometheus chocolate cake with crème anglaise or the tangy Key lime pie. The excellent selection of wines is all-American and reasonably priced. Note there is a three-course prix-fixe dinner for $35. Window seats are best, but you can see the rink from nearly anywhere in the handsome art deco-inspired dining room and tables are large and well spaced for privacy.

The SeaGrill, 19 West 49th Street between Fifth and Sixth Avenues, lower concourse. (212)246-9201. Lunch Monday through Friday 11:45 AM to 2:30 PM, dinner Monday through Saturday 5 to 10 PM. $$$

THE SIGN OF THE DOVE

WITHOUT A DOUBT, the Sign of the Dove is the most sentimentally romantic restaurant in town, with mirrors and brick walls and arches, statuary, beautiful table settings, candles, and flowers, flowers everywhere. The renaissance of this restaurant's kitchen has been widely reported, and now the food matches the promise of romance.

The music room, the favorite of many lovers, features wicker chairs and fringed lamp shades. Others prefer the conservatory with its sliding roof and gardenlike setting seductive even at lunch on a spring or summer day when sunlight streams in and rose petals float down through the open roof. In the evening all of the rooms are softly lighted with well-separated tables, the better to carve out a sphere of privacy. Enticing seasonal dishes such as pumpkin and parmesan ravioli made with homemade ricotta, herb chicken with pan-fried dumplings, and roast fennel-crusted bass *must* be followed with one of the restaurant's gorgeous desserts. The wine list is impressive and fairly priced, so do treat yourself to a selection. If cost is a concern, there is a two-course prix-fixe lunch for $20 and a three-course for $25; for dinner a three-course prix-fixe pretheater dinner is $30. Also for less expensive, more casual dining go to the café/bar up front where you can get close to each other and also listen to live jazz nightly.

The Sign of the Dove, 1110 Third Avenue at East 65th St. (212)861-8080. Lunch Tuesday through Friday noon to 2:30 PM. Dinner Monday through Friday 6 to 11 PM, Saturday 6 to 11:30 PM, Sunday 6 to 10 PM. The bar is open until 1 or 2 AM. Weekend brunch 11:30 AM to 3:30 PM. $$$$+

SONIA ROSE

YOU MIGHT EASILY PASS BY without noticing this small storefront restaurant were it not for the table set for two set on a raised platform in the window. To those who know it, Sonia Rose is a romantic gem located a bit out of the way in an area called Little India. The fact that you must ring to enter is the first clue that dining here is special. The restaurant is long and narrow with only 11 tables, each of which is graced with a candle and roses. It has a charming intimacy with small touches after you're seated, like a warm moist towel to cleanse your hands, that serve to put you in the right frame of mind no matter how hard a day you've had. The eclectic French menu offers a delightful choice of interesting dishes. The menu changes daily, with exceptional seasonal fare flavorfully prepared and beautifully rendered. There is a wonderful $21 three-course prix-fixe lunch that includes a delectable dessert sampler, making Sonia Rose a good choice for an out-of-the-way midweek lunch rendezvous, although it does lose some of its romantic glow in daylight. Dinner is also prix fixe, three courses for $33, and there is nary an empty table all evening, so make sure to reserve in advance if you have a special evening in mind.

Sonia Rose, 132 Lexington Avenue between East 28th and East 29th Streets. (212)545-1777. Lunch Tuesday through Sunday noon to 2 PM Dinner daily 6 PM to 10 PM. $$$

TAVERN ON THE GREEN

HOW AMAZING that this opulent building was a sheepfold housing 200 sheep and a shepherd from 1870 to 1934, at which time the sheep were sent across the bridge to Prospect Park and the first restaurant opened on the premises. Warner LeRoy is the magician who created this fantasy of a dining area within New York's official backyard in 1976. It is one of the most joyful and at times truly magical places to dine. The dazzling Crystal Room with its floor-to-ceiling windows filled with Central Park's glorious seasonal vistas is awe-inspiring. The twinkling little white lights in the trees are there from November to May and serve to make the view even more breathtaking. And if there aren't too many birthday celebrations with waiters singing and large parties of tourists with flashbulbs a-popping, the two of you will be enchanted. To avoid the latter, go for a late lunch or dinner and then dawdle over your coffee and dessert. If you are lucky enough to be in the Crystal Room when it starts to snow or even when the park has a fresh coating of white, you will find yourself in a matchless wonderland.

The outdoor garden, a captivating place to dine on a warm mid-summer evening, is one of the most bucolic settings you can find within Manhattan Island's confines, and in summer you can even dance under the stars (see #62). As for the food, the new chef, Patrick Clark, is now making the menu as dazzling as the surroundings with dishes such as risotto with lobster and red peppers; roasted duck; and Moroccan-style barbecued salmon on a bed of savory cabbage.

Tavern on the Green, in Central Park, Central Park West at West 67th Street. (212)873-3200. Lunch Monday through Friday 11:30 AM to 3:45 PM. Dinner Monday through Thursday 5 PM to midnight, Friday and Saturday until 12:45 AM, Sunday 5:30 to 11:00 PM. Weekend

brunch 10 AM to 3:30 PM. From May through September Tuesday through Thursday and Sunday 9 AM to 1 AM, Friday and Saturday until 2 AM there is dancing to live music in the garden. $$

TERRACE RESTAURANT

ONLY SIXTEEN STORIES HIGH, but by virtue of its Upper West Side location the Terrace with its dramatic views of the George Washington Bridge, its necklace of lights twinkling in the distance, the Hudson River, and the New Jersey Palisades, is shamelessly romantic. The elegant room sparkles in the dim glow of candlelight, each table is set with fine china and a single red rose, live harp music fills the air, and in winter a fire crackles in the fireplace. The overall effect is irresistible, especially if you are in love with each other and with the city. The main dining room faces north to the George Washington Bridge, and eastward on a clear evening you can see all the way to Long Island Sound. The greenhouse dining area faces south. The classic French fare is a delightful surprise considering the view; try the fine prix-fixe sampler menu. The staff is professional and unobtrusive, you will be happy to hear, so you can fully appreciate your meal, the surroundings, and each other. In good weather this is worth a trip uptown even just to have a cocktail or dessert and coffee on the outdoor roof-top terrace, where the view, especially in the late afternoon and evening, is breathtaking.

The Terrace, Butler Hall, 400 West 119th Street near Morningside Drive. (212)666-9490. Lunch Tuesday through Friday noon to 3:30 PM. Dinner Tuesday through Thursday 6 to 10 PM, Friday and Saturday until 10:30 PM. $$$$

Vivolo

VIVOLO is an inviting, unassuming spot where a romantic evening and consistently good Italian fare can be yours at moderate prices—what a relief. Located in a century-old brownstone on the Upper East Side, the downstairs dining room with fireplace is clubby; the upstairs is more like an intimate dining salon. The latter, with its high ceilings, mirrors, and fresh flowers, lends itself to leisurely fireside dining. My favorite place to sit at lunch is in the small dining area at the front, when you can have it nearly all to yourself. The prix-fixe lunch and dinner at Vivolo are excellent buys.

Vivolo, 140 East 74th Street between Lexington and Third Avenues. (212)737-3533. Lunch Monday through Friday noon to 3 PM, dinner Monday through Saturday 5 to 11:15 PM. Jacket required. $$

The Water Club

LITERALLY ON THE EAST RIVER, the Water Club is actually two barges anchored at the water's edge. The view is quite spectacular, especially in the evening when a window seat in the glass-enclosed tiered main dining room offers expansive views of the river, both south and north. The regional American fare, with its emphasis on seafood, and a superior wine selection complement the surroundings. Choose American red snapper with lobster dumplings, basil-crusted yellowfin tuna, and fresh lobster from the restaurant's tank; for carnivores there's a great prime sirloin steak. There is a three-course prix-fixe lunch for $19.95 and dinner for $35.

In warm weather you can opt to soak up the view with a

drink and/or a light meal on the outside terrace on the upper deck (although the sound of the traffic on the adjacent FDR Drive may be a distraction). But in winter the best place for the two of you to get cozy is in the wood-paneled piano bar with its glowing fireside hearth. It's a popular spot well past midnight.

Water Club, East River at 30th Street between the 23rd Street exit of the FDR and East 34th Street. (212)683-3333. Lunch Monday through Friday noon to 2:30 PM. Dinner Monday through Saturday 5:30 to 11 PM, Sunday until 10 PM. Sunday brunch buffet 11:30 AM to 2:30 PM. The bar is open until 1 or 2 AM. $$$$

THE WATER'S EDGE

165)

THE WATER'S EDGE is an inspired choice for dinner on a clear evening, and thanks to its gratis riverboat water shuttle it is literally eight minutes from East 34th Street in Manhattan. The boat shuttle is a charming way to arrive at this lovely, rather formal restaurant located on a barge moored close to the Queensboro Bridge. With its sparkling East River and midtown-Manhattan panorama from a window table in the spacious glass-enclosed dining room and the open-air deck, it's just made for romance, especially at sunset and late in the evening. But that's not the only reason to come to the Water's Edge. The creative contemporary American cooking and the service are more than enough reason to cross the river. Specialty dishes include fricassee of wild mushrooms, roast Maine lobster with shallot confit and roast rack of lamb with basil potato purée and garlic chips. The six-course prix fixe ($65) for dinner is a standout. There's live piano music nightly from 7 to 11 PM, and a fireplace glows in the cocktail lounge in winter. What more could anyone desire, besides each other?

Water's Edge, 44th Drive at the East River, Long Island City, Queens. (718)482-0033. Lunch Monday through Friday noon to 3 PM, dinner Monday through Saturday 6 to 11 PM. Complimentary river shuttle from 6 PM. Jacket required. $$$$+

INDEX

171

176

177